I0159349

RAISING A

PROVERB 31

Woman:

Self-Esteem, Self-Worth, Self-Discovery of a young woman in today's time

A compilation by

LaTracey Copeland Hughes

PURPOSEFUL
PUBLISHING & CONSULTING

"Your Success is OUR Purpose"

Raising A Proverb 31 Woman: Self-Esteem, Self-Worth, Self-Discovery of a young woman in today's time

By LaTracey Copeland Hughes

Published by Purposeful Publishing & Consulting

www.RaisingAProverb31Woman.com

Copyright ©2014 –Purposeful Publishing & Consulting, a subsidiary of Purposeful DIVA Enterprises, LLC, All Rights Reserved. No part of this publication may be reproduced, stored in retrieval system or transmitted in any form or by any means, electronic, mechanical, photocopying, recording or otherwise, without the written permission of the publisher.

The publisher gratefully acknowledges the many individuals who granted Purposeful Publishing and Consulting permission to reprint the cited materials.

Complied by: LaTracey Copeland Hughes
Interior design: LaTracey Copeland Hughes
Editing: Krissti Bryant
ISBN: 978-0615976617

RAISING A PROVERB 31

Woman:

Self-Esteem, Self-Worth, Self-Discovery of a young woman in today's time

A compilation by

LaTracey Copeland Hughes

www.RaisingAProverb31Woman.com

Acknowledgements

I would like to acknowledge every woman for taking this huge step of faith to overcome all odds and walk together hand by hand while Raising A Proverb 31 Woman within.

Dedication:

First, giving all honor and praise to my Heavenly Father for from which all blessings flow I am forever grateful. To Preston, my husband, for your love and support as I walk out my God-given purpose with you by my side. Our children, Azuria, Isaiah, Razaria, and Purpose thank you for sharing your mommy with the world.

All proceeds from this book will go to fund Capstone Experience, Inc., 501c3 nonprofit organization. Please visit www.capstoneexperience.org for more information or to donate.

Table of Contents

Meet the Contributors

Meet the Author

Forward

Why the title, Raising A Proverb 31 Woman: Self-Esteem, Self-Worth and Self-Discovery of a young woman? The biblical term of Proverbs 31 is noted about the virtuous character of a woman which is the foundation of this book, but using the term Proverb is a single term. A profound beginning to this journey as a woman of God is stated plainly in the bible but I struggled with the idea of living up to this standard daily.

When I realized that I wasn't alone in the journey, I went into prayer to seek God on why I felt so alone in this process. Embracing it through my tears, the wisdom I received was that I wasn't alone in this and the mantle on my life was to solicit the testimonies of my fellow sisters young and old as we rise up the Proverb 31 Woman within ourselves.

Women from all over the world accepted the call and transparently shared their real, raw unedited stories to help another young woman in the journey to purpose. The marketplace has no place for those that will selfishly go through things without getting the wisdom from the elders.

This book is only the beginning. It is a major part of the Proverbs 31 Woman Project, which our quest is to strengthen the community and globally, we are recruiting strong, positive female role models to help empower, uplift and motivate women to achieve their vision of tomorrow.

I pray you are blessed by the lessons as well as the challenges from each contributor as they reach you right where you are in your passage to Raising A Proverb 31 Woman.

Clothed in Virtue

~

At the age of 3, my mother chose crack over me

From that point on I lost my identity

And in crept insecurities

It wasn't until a divorce and a baby

Did my self-worth become a reality?

And that it wasn't much

I mean my own mother didn't even want me

I went through so much in between

From abuse, depression, to molestation, and alcohol use

But it didn't erase the memories

Or stop me from hearing my mother's excuses

Of why she was never there

Or why she gave me her crack pipe to share

Or why she didn't call me on my birthdays

Or why she just up a disappeared for over 5 years

Or why my new mommy hated it me

So I had hate for them both

It was a catastrophe that

At the age of 3, my mother chose crack over me

Did she ever consider how her decision of irresponsibility would affect me?

How it would leave me completely alone

Extremely lost within

How it would leave me filling my life with voids to replace her

How it would have me falling in and out of love

How it would lead me to abuse

How it would leave me to attempt to take my life

How self-mutilation gave me comfort

How I never looked in the mirror because I didn't think I was pretty enough

I just could not understand why she didn't want to be my mother

All I wanted her to simply say is I love you

A simple kiss on the forehead would do

But no, at the age of 3, my mother chose crack over me

Once I understood that this all had to be

It took me on a path to self-discovery

I fell in love with a man who loved me unconditionally

Who gave His only begotten Son?

To die for me and set me free of all the pain, and all the hurt

To some day understand my self-worth

To no longer be in bondage of my past

No longer did my pain keep me masked

From the lies I told myself

From the bad choices I made

I finally understood

He knew the plans he had for me

He was simply preparing me for my Destinee

A little girl who loves freely

A gift that gave me insight on who I was really called to be

A plan to help me on my journey of building self-esteem, self-worth, and self-discovery

As my Father, He loved me

And knew that my strength from this

Would lead me to

My purpose

To serve

To bring Him glory

By sharing my story

My path to self-esteem, self-worth, and self-discovery took me on a journey of feeling unloved and searching for it in all the wrong places, to finding love and forgiveness through my Father so that finally I could give unconditional love to my daughter.

For every woman young or old, you want to feel loved, especially from the very ones that are supposed to love you. I found myself searching for love in relationships. I remember putting myself in dangerous situations just for the attention. To include: being promiscuous, fighting, running away fun home, drinking, and being extremely rebellious. I left my father's home for days at a time, catching the Greyhound bus anywhere I could to just get way and even got into cars with strangers.

My perception of love was distorted. In my mind rejection and abandonment were normal. I saw no purpose in being loyal or staying in relationships because I lacked the capacity to trust. I expected to be abandoned, disrespected, and rejected. Then came who I thought was my night and shining armor, a man I thought I would spend the rest of my life with. Not understanding that broken girls, ultimately become wounded women. Therefore, I pursued marriage although I was still in a place of hurt. There was every possible sign to indicate to me that this man was not my helpmate but I ignored myself to avoid being alone. My mind began telling me I was getting older and I needed to start my career and family right then and right there. So though this man lied, cheated, and stole from my soul, I felt he loved me because he apologized sincerely and stayed around.

Then pregnancy came within 7 months of being married and my life was turned completely upside down. He literally woke up one morning and decided I was not the woman for him so he left. Now I am a new mother, unemployed, and separated. I began blaming myself and my past for this tragedy and this landed me in a state of depression. My newborn baby was not being mothered properly. I had no energy mentally, spiritually, or emotionally, so I neglected her. In my eyes, I had become my mother. What little girl doesn't want to be held by her mother? A generational curse repeated itself. Will I live this way? So I begin to pray. I knew God, but I didn't trust Him either. Where was He? At this point I sent every prayer I could to get out of this state of mind and He quickly answered.

Laying in my bed, my phone rings, and it's my grandmother. She said, "Hi baby, this is your grandmother and I have some great news, we found your mother." At this point it had been over 15 years since I last heard from her. All I could do is cry. So my grandmother gave me her number. So I wrote it down and prayed. Why now? Well as I began reading and spending more time with the Lord, I began to understand that I needed to forgive my mother before I could be a mother. God opened up that opportunity one day and I called. It was great hearing from her and I felt so free after our discussion. In an effort to completely heal, it was recommended through a friend that I seek some counsel. This was the best advice ever. I got the help and let go of the pain and the hurt. My perception on motherhood changed completely. I understood that God gave me a give of life and sent that gift to restore my soul. Therefore, I began seeking Him even more and He showed His unchanging love through a child. She is the joy of my life. She is my strength. She is everything to me and our bond is like nothing I've ever experience from a human on earth. It was through His love that I found love.

My message to young women is that you are only defined by what you allow to define you. Your self-esteem, self-worth, and self-discovery are in knowing that you were created by God and He loves you more than anything. He created you before the foundation of the world and knew how to mold you and make you for His glory. He knew you before you were implanted in your mother's womb. You are fearfully and wonderfully made. His love is unfailing. Everything you endure is not for you but to help someone else. You are worth it. Your of your greatest hurts will come from those you love. On the other hand, your greatest success is a result of the very things that caused the most hurt and pain. Your experiences make you who you are and will drive you into your purpose. God will never give you something to great for you to handle.

Challenge:

I challenge young women is to love the Lord thy God with all your heart, with all your heart, all your soul, with your entire mind, and with all your strength. Know that you're created for greatness and never settle for less. Seek Him first before you make any decisions. Spend time talking to Him and studying His word. Surround yourself among others who are Godly, positive, and inspire you to be better than you are. Forgive those who hurt you because un-forgiveness will paralyze you. Finally, give God Glory for all things by sharing your story. Sharing your story will bring healing to others.

The Proverbs 31 Woman who is clothed with strength and dignity; can laugh at the days to come because she understands that she can do all things through Christ who gives her strength. She knows how to pray and trust God through it all. She has dignity because she understands that what she goes through works together for her good. She can walk boldly before His throne of grace and receive forgiveness for her insufficiencies. She can forgive and not harness hate because she knows how to release her pain. She can laugh at days to come because of the days that she left behind to fully trust and depend on Him.

Lakita Thompson

Proverbs 31:10-31
Women aren't created
without a cost

Capturing Virtue

In today's society there are many things that can capture the eye as well as your heart. Fame, wealth, beauty and social status just to name a few? These are all things that can cause you to be tricked into thinking that they are more important than a relationship with God. For many, the beauty portrayed in magazines have many young women feeling like unless they look this way they are not beautiful. The pictures are false representations of how a real woman should be. I know for myself, they fooled me. As a young girl growing up, I wanted to look like, be like and act like what I saw on TV or what was presented in magazines. At that time for me, that was the life, they were popular as well as beautiful and they had anything that money could buy. These things were very appealing to me and I wanted to have all of that. Why? Well for me, I saw myself as not attractive, I wore glasses and I had to wear others hand me downs and I was slightly over-weight. In looking at those women, they seemed to have it all together and everyone loved them and wanted to be them, this was my heart's desire.

Over the course of my childhood I fantasized about being these women, and having people love me and wanting to be me, just as I did them. This caused me to make many terrible decisions and mistakes. I disobeyed my mother just so that I could fit in and rebelled against authority because I wanted to be accepted. This caused many problems for me as a pre-teen as well as a teenager. But, in doing all of those things, I still had a longing for more; there was still a void in my life. I thought that having friends and name brand cloths would do it, but it only worked for a while and then it was back. The more I bought and spent the worst I actually felt, because after it was all over I was still me, nothing changed that, not the name brand cloths, nor the friends.

Every day I looked in the mirror I was still the same person, just in expensive cloths, after I left my so –called friends I was still the same person. Nothing changed who I was, I would look at other teens and wished to be them, but it never happened. I was still me, there was nothing I could do to change that, or so I thought. After graduation, I went away to the Army and having the opportunity to see the world and to be able to do some of the things I desired to do, I was still not satisfied. I spent money like it was water, I would get paid on Monday and be broke on Wednesday with nothing to show for it except a few cloths and shoes. I did not realize at the time that I was headed down a road of destruction. I was about to self-destruct. I was getting in trouble in the Army, and they had threated to put me out, but I did not care, I was going to be me.

Well I was me and they put me out, so there I was back at home. It wasn't until I was back and I saw that things were still the same, nothing had changed, all my so called friends were still doing the same thing, and I wanted more. The going out, the rebelling, the sneaking around was old to me. I wanted more, I had messed up a chance of a lifetime, and I wanted to get my life back on track. I had seen what wanting to be someone else got you, nowhere. I wanted to be me and get my life on track. I no longer wanted to be like someone else I wanted to be me.

I came across an old friend that I took for granted before I left, and she and I began to talk. It was at that time that she began to tell me her story and I was like wow, this sounds like me. We were both feeling the same way and struggling with the same thing, but to ashamed to tell anyone, so we covered it up and faked our way through it. For the first time in my life, I was able to be "real", that was a great feeling. I no longer wanted to be like the models in the magazines, or the actresses on TV. I just wanted to be me, the one God created me to be.

My friend's mom took us under her wing to help us be good Christian young ladies. I was now living a life that I had heard about before but never knew it could happen to me. I was able to open up and be honest about the things I had done and the lies I had told. I was able to be set free. I took some time, but I was willing to allow the work to be done so that I could be all that God created me to be. I soon realized that as they say, "everything that glimmers isn't gold".

The life I was so longing to have and wishing for was not the life God intended for me to have. He created me special and unique, there is only one of me and He did that for a reason. It was up to me to find out that reason. I was not supposed to be like someone else, I was supposed to be who He made me to be. All those things that captured my attention and distracted me were just that distractions, they were not for me. God had and has better. So from that day forward, I learned to love God, and trust Him and to know that He knows what's best for me. I also learned to be me, and love me and not want to be anyone else other than who God made me to be. This is a lesson that I am still learning even today. The things of this world will soon pass way, but only what you do for God will last. Beauty and material things will get old and fade and go out of style, but the things God has planned and prepared for you will never get old. The lesson I learned and want to pass along to you is to find out who you are in God and love you for who He made you to be. Personal identify shouldn't be in things or people, but it is in God. Things will wear out and get old, people will walk out on you and leave you by yourself, but God will never leave you and trust He will never get old. The challenge I have for you is to learn more about God. Trust when you do, you will learn more about who you really are and not what others say you are. Be Blessed.

Leslie Epps Wallace

Becoming A Virtuous Woman

Growing up in a very spiritual family this has been one of the scriptures that I would always think about. I've always wanted to be that virtuous woman. A woman that is a pillar in the community and who is a loving caring, compassionate wife and mother. Unfortunately life dealt me some blows that I believed that knocked me out of the race to be that woman. My father died when I was fourteen. My mother tried her best to maintain a sense of normalcy for us, but it was hard.

We were homeless for two years and being the oldest of six children I had to help out a lot and take care of my younger siblings while my mother worked. Now while dealing with my father's death and being homeless we discovered that I had breast tumors. By the grace of God they were benign; however, I still had to have surgery to remove them. This caused me to miss a lot of school. Once I was healed and well enough to return to school I was told that I would not graduate with my class on time. This was a tough thing for me to accept. After all that I'd been through I wondered when, was I going to hear some good news. The following year my mother was blessed with a beautiful home for us and I was able to get back on track to graduating with my class (which I did with hard work).

As I began to get my life on track my mother died leaving me to raise my two youngest siblings. Dealing with her death was the hardest thing that I have ever had to go through. I sank into a deep depression and withdrew from everyone I knew, yet I maintained a poker face for the sake of my siblings because they looked to me for their strength. Meanwhile I was dying inside. I had given up on myself and I had given up on God.

One day my pastor came by and my house was completely dark. Blinds drawn, lights off and the doors closed. She came in and prayed for me and said that it was time for me to get out of the darkness and step into the light. After she opened the blinds and doors the sunshine came right through. The sun had never seemed that bright to me until that day. I got up, I cried and I asked God to forgive me for turning my back on Him.

From that day forward I decided to live in the light. I met my husband not too longer after "seeing the light" and I became a mother. I will admit I never thought that I would be able to say those things. Today I am still in my pursuit of being that virtuous woman, but with the mentality of I can and determination of I will. While I have only been on this journey for two years I still have the challenge of shaking old habits. For instance one of my weaknesses is procrastination. I combat this habit by just doing whatever I need to do once it comes to mind instead of waiting. It was hard, but with consistency I am overcoming it.

The lesson that I have learned is that no matter what you go through it is in preparation for something great. You have to deal with tough situations in order to develop your own strength and character. I had to learn to love myself again and I had to believe that I was capable of reaching my dreams. I had to encourage myself daily. There were times when I would fall off, but I had to pick myself up and try again. There is no time limit on reaching your dreams! As long as you have God as the head of your life and you surround yourself with genuine people who care for you, you will get to your purpose in life. My journey continues.

Trevva Evans

Strength & Honor

As the middle child growing up with 1 sister and 3 brothers, life has been full of experiences for me. At the age of 16 I started dating a guy around town who was most known for his basketball skills. He was 3 years older than me and though a lot of people thought he was arrogant and cocky, he didn't seem to act that way when we were around each other. Things began to progress and by the age of 17 my senior year in high school I found out I was pregnant. I was in total denial. The funny thing was a week before that I had actually went to a clinic to start birth control. When I told him he was shocked, but happy to say the least but I was concerned because he was set to go overseas to Sweden and play basketball, but not only that I was terrified to tell my mom and dad.

When I told my mom she instantly said I couldn't have the baby. We grew up in church and I couldn't believe she was saying this. After a few weeks she sat us both down and apologized for her rash behavior and told us this was our choice to make. For me she told me that all my dreams of becoming a model would be done because children change your body and it's a big responsibility. Well we came to the decision I would have the baby. At that time I had had numerous of friends throughout high school that had abortions and for me I just couldn't do it, So I went on with my pregnancy and it was wonderful.

He put off going to play ball until after the baby was born. He spoiled me rotten ,I mean catered to me even with phone calls at 3am because I had cravings and he would run out and get whatever I needed. My daughter was born 5 days earlier then my due date given and she was everything I prayed for in a child. I never knew I could experience so much joy. The good thing was that I was always smart and driven so I thought ahead when it came to school so I took summer school classes the year prior and I graduated early due to having more credits than needed. I was set to walk the stage 3 months after her birth and I did just that.

Here I am a high school graduate and a 3month old daughter, in my head now saying what to do next because yes I did gain weight but lucky I didn't have major stretch marks because in the back of my mind I knew I wanted to be a model and or be in the entertainment business of some range . Watching many friends go off to college I was faced with reality much sooner than I ever thought.

Then it happened my mom said OK you're grown enough to have a child your grown enough to live on your own. She didn't kick me out, but she said I needed to look for a place of my own. My daughter's father was in the process of leaving for Sweden too for a few months. I didn't mind because I believed in him and his dream and I always told him no matter what happens between us please be a father to your daughter and he made the promise he would. So my older sister had a child also so me and her found our first apartment and moved in together. Things were great I enrolled in the local college not having any idea what to major in because I never really saw myself in college.

Her father returned after a few months and thing were good for a while, but then something changed in him. He now had the attitude of I'm not ready to be a father. He gave up on his dream and became a drug dealer and was in and out of jail. He began cheating on me and was not taking care of his responsibilities as a father. After this I was devastated, lost, and confused. I remembered picking up a mini bible my godmother had given me and begin reading the passages of Matthews. When I got to 7:7-11 I begin to read "Ask, and it will be given to you; seek, and you will find; knock, and it will be opened to you. For everyone who asks receives, and the one who seeks finds, and to the one who knocks it will be opened…" I reread this a few times and found myself on my knees praying to God for direction, praying for healing of my heart from being torn at the hands of someone who I thought loved me and my daughter, praying for forgiveness of getting pregnant without being married, praying that he would help me move on without bitterness and asking him to lead me to what my purpose is in life. I cried, I cried and boy did I cry. I tell you what when I got up off my knees I felt renewed and put it in his hands. Needless to say my daughters' father had decided to move to Texas.

It really didn't matter because at that point he had stopped providing support for her a long time ago. He had got to the point if I didn't want to be with him in that way he didn't want to be involved with her. He told me that I was too demanding and expected things from him just because I had given him a child but the truth is even though he was the older one my daughter changed me and I grew up and he didn't. What I expected of him was to be a man and be there for his child as he promised but that didn't happen. And the system failed me, I went to the government and asked for child support and can you believe they ordered him to pay $5 a month, yes I said $5 a month and that was only when he was able to keep a job but time went on and I found someone else who was there for me and my child unconditionally. Then one day I went to a talk show and was an audience member with one of my good friends who wanted to be a model also ironically and I was approached after the show and was asked to become one of the talk show models to perform skits for the show.

For me I began to live out some of my dream, being on television modeling and acting was the jump start I needed to start my journey in fulfilling my dream and that was just the beginning .I was modeling and went back to college eventually I moved from Illinois to Atlanta, GA were more opportunities began to fall in my lap. I then was able to meet people I never thought I could, acting in movies, doing fashion shows, magazine spreads and etc. I later found myself working a wonderful full time job which I love and am still able to act and model at leisure. I have a boss who fully supports me in continuing to fulfill my dream and goals.

 God made a way for me at 17 years old to have a child and be a single parent and take care of my child and also allow me to fulfill some of my dreams without compromising who I am or what I stand for as a woman and a mother. I look at life, as nothing is impossible if you ask God. Tell him what you need and what you want and if you seek him you shall find. I learned a couple of lessons from this experience. Thou I would never regret my child ,I tell young woman whenever I can that not only is safe sex important but you should definitely try to wait until God sends the man that is for you and if you can ,wait until you are married. That union between a man and woman I know now is sacred, And so is your body which is your temple. The world we live in today promotes promiscuity amongst our young females. The teen pregnancy rate was recently at an all-time high. Having children at a young age can propose a lot of obstacles but for me with prayer and belief God brought me through it and still moving mountains for me. He gave me the strength to continue to be strong and a very delicate moment in my life. Whenever there is doubt talk to him, pray and he will give you all of the strength that you need to keep on going no matter what the problem is, He is able.

Toya Sherie Gathings

Knowing My Worth

"So Candace, who do you want to be when you grow up?" said my 7th grade English Teacher in a very matter-of-fact yet curious tone. "When I grow up, I want to be an attorney!" I replied, as I sat in my chair with my chest poked out and head held high in pride. My English Teacher wasn't satisfied with that answer and she continued to probe; "Why is this career choice?" I took a deep breath and replied confidently; "Well I know that as an attorney I will be able to use my debate skills for good and assist people who don't know their rights or the Law." As I concluded, my teacher nodded her head in agreement and proceeded to question the next student.

At a very young age, 12 to be exact, I was very sure of myself, confident and enthused about life and what I could offer it. I was also serious about my studies and hearing my name announced during Honor Roll Assemblies was the norm. My life at home was pretty exciting day to day seeing as though I shared a room with my two younger brothers and we always managed to get into something creative. I was in a routine of doing my own thing until one day while in school I suddenly realized that I didn't have many friends, I talked differently than my classmates and I noticed the snickers behind my back during lunch and recess.

Ok, let me stop right here, I'm trying to be politically correct and go easy on the things that have happened in my life and attempt to paint a more "decent" picture, yet the reality of it is, if I don't convey my story to you in its most pure, uncut form, I could possibly be depriving you from having preview to a journey that may prevent you from making the same mistakes that I made. I could sum everything up about my life and my poor choices into a few words; Fatherless, Abandoned, Afraid, Left-Out, Un-worthy and Misguided. However, these words don't tell you much about what I went through, do they? Of course not, because even if these words are the root for some of the experiences that I took part in, they don't convey the options that I always had despite my circumstances. Some self-inflicted and others due to my environment and the company kept.

As I mentioned above, at a very young age I knew what I wanted to do with my life and how to get there but things all fell apart for me when I adopted the desire to want to fit in and attract attention. Initially it began with the change in the way I talked; instead of speaking properly I chose to use slang and profanity to express myself. Doing this made me part of the crowd, I mean, everyone else was doing it. Besides, I got sick of being picked on for using proper grammar, as long as I dropped the twang in my voice when I got home and spoke with my Mom, I was fine. Then as the months went by I noticed that all of the girls around me had boyfriends, so of course I wanted one too. So I started hanging out the coolest guy in the 7th grade, they called him "Chello", I proceeded thinking that since everyone liked him, they would like me too. This sort of behavior continued as I moved on to High School, I was once again the cute girl, but still the nerd nevertheless. I didn't have the usual wardrobe of a stylish inner city freshman student. See, I came from a single parent household so I didn't have the luxury of wearing the latest name brand clothes and shoes, forget about it, my brothers and I were simply pleased to get new tennis shoes at Christmas. I felt the need to fit in, only this time, I went out and got a job at the age of 14. Some would say that this was wise, mature and even commendable but in reality what this did was sidetrack me from my studies and grow my love and affection for money and clothes to an excessive degree. I began to find my worth in wearing the newest clothes, getting the envious looks from some and compliments from others. Instead of focusing on what I wanted and needed to do in order to reach my future goals: I began studying the "popular girls" around me and I suddenly did everything they did, oh but in a different size or color, of course.

By the time I reached my senior year of High School I had the reputation of "Pretty Candi with the Red Hair", yes, I had red hair. I held my head high at the thought that I was well-known, liked and thought as quite attractive. However, what my classmates didn't know was internally, I had no idea where I was going, who I was and what I was good at, well except for styling hair, I was very good at that. My association with my self-worth and outward appearances continued to magnify.

I graduated High School with a mediocre grade point average, a far cry from the honors accolades that I had grown accustomed to only a few years prior in grade school. Well, right after high school "Pretty Candi" saw how much attention she gained from the opposite sex, only this time these guys weren't those in my peer group. I found myself partying in 21+ nightclubs and dating men who might I add had intentions as honest as their professions, which needless to say, "street pharmacists" weren't honest at all. Being associated with guys who sold drugs opened up a completely different world for me, I no longer had to worry about money or shoes or clothes, as this was now freely at my disposal. However, in exchange for the shopping sprees and my first car being bought for me at age 19, I saw a lot and put myself in situations that I never thought I'd be in.

Have you noticed that I didn't mention college, yet? Well, that's because I sampled higher education for a brief year and allowed myself to be preoccupied by a lifestyle that seemed to give me the type of gratification that I had never previewed before. It sounds fun right? Shopping, Cars, Clothes, Trips, Yacht Parties, Clubbing, right? I mean after all, isn't that what we all want and work hard for? Wrong, what I was truly getting myself into was a world of darkness. Imagine not being able to sleep thinking that someone would invade your home at any time to rob or kill your boyfriend, imagine jumping up in the middle of the night while holding a loaded gun with fear swelling in your heart at the thought that you might need to pull the trigger to defend yourself. Or how about imagining how it feels to know that a man's sole purpose for you is to transport the illegal substances that has afforded your frivolous lifestyle; and every state trooper that drives by you on the expressway could potentially pull you over, find what you have hidden in your vehicle, thus ending any options for a future you thought possible. Or what about helping the one you so-called "love" dodge law enforcement. These are all scenarios that I knew too well and have lived, all while watching my soul deteriorate and the sparkle in my eye diminish.

I can speak to you now as I look back on my life and tell you that all of these circumstances and experiences were brought upon me for two reasons:

1. I refused to be myself (learn, grow and embrace her)

2. I looked for love and validation in the most fallible creature on Earth, human beings.

Having a poor view of myself caused me to disassociate with the things in life that could set me apart and build a great future. Education being most important, whether it's formal or informal, gaining knowledge and pursuing your goals will always keep you on the right path and decrease distractions. The fact of the matter was that often times instead of looking within to see what we truly love and want we try to fit in and I'll tell you, there is NO way to fit comfortably in a one-size fits all life, as a matter of fact, there is no such thing. What I have also grown to realize is that my increasing need to be loved or feel love from material things and people, separated me from feeling the love that was always there all along; the unconditional love of God. If in my time of feeling inferior, depressed, unwanted, lonely and rejected, I would have made the decision to turn it all over to God and let him guide me, I could have avoided much heartache. Also, forgiving the Father that left me as a child and pardoning the relationships that pained me would have prevented me long ago from reliving the same cycle over and over again. These trials only served the purpose of standing in the way of me being who I was truly destined to be. I was in my own way!

Yet, as they say, hindsight is 20/20, I truly believe that. Especially, seeing how I am now able to express to you my struggles, shortcomings and weaknesses in hopes that you will look at all of your options and choose a better path. So if in some way this reaches you and makes you think twice about following the crowd, hiding drugs for your boyfriend, dropping out of school or hanging on to hurt, un-forgiveness and the fear of rejection, well then I guess my journey was well worth it, in order to guide you towards better. Now I'm sure you're thinking, now what does this have to do with being a Proverbs 31 Woman, well here is how this all relates.

In the book of Proverbs, the Bible describes a strong, wise, multi-faceted woman who protects her home, guards her heart, is ladylike in her ways, stays focused on profitable things and she exudes good character. Many people read this story in the Bible and think that the

Proverbs 31 woman is a woman that had to have been raised to be this way since birth, or groomed over much time by other women, as Esther was. However, who I see the Proverbs 31 woman to be is the woman who is willing to evolve into complete womanhood using her past as a stepping-stone to mold her future and protect others. I see the Proverbs 31 woman as any woman who has completely submitted her life to God and allows him to use her; the Proverbs 31 woman is a woman who is proud to share her testimony. The Proverbs 31 woman is a woman that will tell you the truth in love in order to help you reflect, grow and make the best decisions for your life. The Proverbs 31 woman is the woman that I want to see you become, the woman of noble character, the woman who knows herself, the direction for her life and trusts God to lead her to her purpose.

I will share with you my favorite verses from Proverbs 31 (ERV):

16-18 She looks at land and buys it. She uses the money she has earned and plants a vineyard. She works very hard. She is strong and able to do all of her work. She works late into the night to make sure that her business earns profit.

25-27 She is a strong person and people respect her. She looks to the future with confidence. She speaks with wisdom and teaches others to be loving and kind. She oversees the care of her house. She is never lazy

30 Grace and beauty can fool you, but a woman who respects the Lord should be praised.

10 ...She is worth far more than Jewels.

Now you may look at this and see that it is out of sequence at the very end, well I saved the tenth verse for last. I did this so that if you don't remember anything else is, you will remember that: YOU ARE WORTH FAR MORE THAN JEWELS. I will say this again; YOU ARE WORTH FAR MORE THAN JEWELS. As girls and as women we often forget our value and we associate our worth with things of the world, but the Bible has clearly stated that YOU ARE WORTH FAR MORE THAN JEWELS. So the next time someone tries to belittle you or make you feel unimportant or irrelevant, think on this. The next time some young boy tries to buy you a new pair of shoes or a purse or whatever in exchange for your body, think on this. And the next time you find yourself comparing your life, skin color, hair, grades, size or smile to your classmates or best friend, think on this: YOU ARE WORTH MORE THAN JEWELS. So now that we know that God has determined our worth for us in His Word, let's take a look at our responsibilities.

Challenge:

As a young woman, make sure that in everything that you do, you seek God first! Secondly, respect your parents, elders, school officials and any person in authority, being able to honor your leaders is the first step in becoming a great leader. Additionally, keep in mind that the most beautiful characteristic that you can have is confidence and staying committed to your morals and beliefs, being pretty is ok but true eternal beauty comes from within.

Trust me, I know firsthand; this life and the people around you will offer you many alternative ways and shortcuts to reach a successful life, empty compliments and broken promises but remaining true to yourself will get you very far, perseverance and staying on course will attract all that your heart desires. Displaying good manners and staying away from gossip will also show people that your only interest is to speak well of others and do positive things.

Also, remember that a wise young woman doesn't need to express herself using profanity, you are way too intelligent for that and when you find yourself in a situation where you are at a loss for words or are so angry that you want to use every foul word ever created, simply take a deep breath and say nothing. Silence is always an option and most times this gives you time to digest your feelings before you use words that you may regret or may harm you later.

Also you see that the verses mention; working hard, never being lazy, earning money and investing. So as a young woman; be sure to work hard in school and always invest in yourself, this means perhaps studying an extra hour to insure that you make honors. Or it may mean saving the money from your part-time job so that you will have money to buy your essentials or books while in college. These practices will allow you to go far in your future; you will blossom into a Proverbs 31 woman who will one day help other young women on their journey.

Now some of you may be asking, "Wait what happened to Candi?" Well, here is what happened: She finally woke up, took the time to grow up, stopped making excuses and accepted responsibility for her life, choices and outcomes. But more importantly, she surrendered her life to Jesus. Am I the 2014 Mother Theresa? No, not by far and I am still making an effort every day to become more Christ-like and truly pursue my God-given purpose through my gifts and talents. Yet, in just a short three years, I have noticed the company that I keep change drastically (for the better) and I have been blessed with numerous opportunities that I thought once before had escaped me. In the most recent year I have developed an even closer relationship with God and a far much less need to be "liked" by everyone.

I have started working more diligently on projects that I once only dreamed about, for example, I began my own blog which afforded me the opportunity to become a published blogger with a Non-Profit Organization in the Northwest Suburbs of Chicago, I have been welcomed to attend many stellar events and speak on platforms that will encourage, inspire and educate youth and the underprivileged and in a short 7 weeks I will finally complete my Bachelor of Science Degree in Entertainment Business. Might I add, my grade point average is trending above a 3.0, see that honors spirit resurfaced, and by the Grace of God I will pursue my Master's Degree in Public Relations this May. So, although the road to getting where I am now, was not a straight path, nor easy, it taught me many valuable lessons. As I continue to aspire toward greatness I encourage you to do the same and remember that ANYTHING meant for your demise can be turned around for your good, with God's hand over your life!

"Formula for Success: Dream Big, Work Hard, Persevere

& most of all: have faith in yourself and God"

-Unknown

Candace Marquez

The Designer's Label

I recall a little girl in New Orleans that was OK and comfortable in her own skin. She embraced the shape of her body, her full lips, the color of her skin and her wide nose, but she felt as though the acceptance of others and what they thought was important too. At times that BUT seemed really big. For her it was her clothing; she did not have name brand items, but she was always presentable, neat and well dressed. She was a friendly youth, she never met a stranger, but if that same friendship was not returned it was difficult for her to understand. She was young and impressionable.

What that young mind did not realized is that putting that much stock into the opinions of others is dangerous. Our peer's voices will always be present, but they are not to be our standard, the measuring stick or the authority by which we govern ourselves. The young one wanted so badly to fit in with her peers. She had not come to the knowledge that things don't make the person. She had not truly understood that differences are a part of growing up; and that differences are a part of life. The young girl did not have a clue, but as time progressed, she finally grasped the concept.

I finally found my strength as an individual, but it only happened when I realized that to truly and completely love myself came as a result of accepting His! Proverbs 31:10-31 speaks of a woman, but her age is not mentioned. She could have been any age, but what we know for sure is that she was a woman who mattered too many. The proverbs 31 woman found security in her own ability, she found it in the people that she loved and that loved her and she found it in the influence that she possessed. She knew who she was and whose she was. She knew that she carried "The designer's label" which made her a virtuous woman by design. A designer is one who devises or executes designs, especially one who creates forms, structures, and patterns, as for a work of art.

In Proverbs 31:13, 18-19, 20, 22, we see her following the characteristic of the Father. The bible says, she was a creator, a maker, a designer and she put her hands to working with bolts of flax and wool, fine linen and beautiful purple silks making garments and tapestries, designing coverings; she had a brand and a market. Her kindness, care and concern for others spoke volumes. People knew her because of her works; her ability to sew was a gift. She was not selfish with her creations; she then in turn sowed her positivity into the lives of others. She did not seek fulfillment from external forces that did not add to her confidence. But rather, she allowed her influences to bless others. She was designed to be selfless.

When I was younger, the importance of His label than that of others was one I had not yet fully embraced. I was too immature to know that His love, ultimately as His daughter, was far more important than any other voice. The labels others attached to me were canceled when I receive the revelation that what He says supersede all others. I challenge you to change the label, the declaration, the decree and your proclamation.

They said, "You are not pretty!" God says, "You are beautiful. The designer made you fearfully and wonderfully."

They said, "Can't" God say "you can."

They put you down and discourage you. God labeled me as encouraged and lifted.

They hurt you! God calls you healed.

They desire to see you in pieces! The Designer's label says, "You are whole."

They choose to lie on you; But God covers you in truth.

They talk about you, gossip and slander your name. God talks to you in a calm gentle voice.

They say that you don't matter! The designer label says,

"Before I formed you in the womb, I knew you. Before you were born, I set you apart for my holy purpose. I appointed you to be a prophet to the nations." Jeremiah 1:5 (GW)

The designer's label says, "For I know the thoughts that I think towards you, saith the LORD, thoughts of peace, and not of evil, to give you an expected end." Jeremiah 29:11 (KJV)

The designer's label says, "How precious also are thy thoughts unto me, O God! How great is the sum of them!" Psalms 139:17 (KJV)

Their love is conditional and changing.

The designer's label says that you are worth it!!! He loves you unconditionally, relentlessly, stubbornly, without wavering, and forever!!!!!!

~

Challenge: Once you embrace the Love of the Father; you can then see what he sees and say what he says. Now that you've got it, cover others; share the Love of the Lord!!!! Use your influence as she did in Proverbs 31. Seek to fill and cover yourself with positive labels that will inspire others. Change your standard. No longer measure yourself by videos, magazines and the validation of others. The fact that they don't see your beauty, your uniqueness, your individuality and what you offer and may add to the world is irrelevant.

Happiness is a label from the designer, wear it!!!! Peace carries the same tag. He paid the ultimate price wear his LOVE; it is a garment that will not ever wear out.

Self-love can only be established when you accept His love!

Montrice J. B. Littleton

Virtuously Unstuck

Imagine someone told you that a verse of scripture could help to give you the courage, motivation, and inspiration to overcome the obstacles in your life: Give her of the fruit of her hands; and let her own works praise her in the gates, 31:10-31. But what can you do by your hands that really make a difference in your lives and those around you? You can be compassionate and generous! Simple! Here are a few easy ideas: try lending a hand to people who are less fortunate by volunteering in an animal shelter or soup kitchen. In fact, whatever you are dealing with in that moment of life will surely disappear against the adversity of those you help. Try planning ahead; a woman who thinks ahead can anticipate her needs and the needs of her family, her friends, and her significant other.

She opened her mouth with wisdom; and in her tongue is the law of kindness. Imagine how simply providing for someone else can also provide for you the strength and love to be unwavering! Imagine sharing your words of wisdom and affection.

But so many times the reason we feel stuck, demotivated, uninspired is because our world is centered on "me". So many times in our own lives, we're holding onto: "my rights, my time, my privacy, my peace of mind, my space." If we live egocentric lives now, we will reap the fruit of our own hands later.

Remember, you may have never considered these before; here are a few reasons why not:

1.   Rejection. It's normal to reject this concept; to reject that image of a perfect woman, it's outdated and unrealistic. We're programmed by our culture to reject this depiction, even for many in the church.

2.   But rejection comes through a real missing, a real piece of the puzzle that we have forgotten: You're not alone! Do you feel like you can't rise up? Do you wish you said all the right and perfect things and made the best decisions – but you didn't? It's OK! When you can't do what god asks by yourself –it's the starting place to

victory! You're not a failure, you've just forgot who is really inside of you, God. He's there for you to lean on, trust, and have faith in. You can relax knowing that a life of faith can help you overcome anything!

3.   Acceptance. When you accept that someone else is there for you to guide you support you, and to stand up when you're not sure you can – everything becomes a possibility. You can get out of the cycle of struggle through acceptance.

There is still a very real place for gospel to apply to the challenges you may face in life and to find the strength to overcome it. For example, being a woman who is virtuous also means being a woman who can manage her resources. This is something you can easily incorporate into your life. But do you feel like you can't get through something: school problems, issues with your friends, poor grades, or even struggles with your parents? Remember that the inner power inside of you is very much alive! But also remember that you have people around you, resources! You have mentors, teachers, pastors, etc. who are available to help you manage your situation. And, if you are someone who looks to be of service to those around you it will always find its way back to you – especially in moments where you need it most. To sum it all up, give and you shall receive; you reap what you sow.

If something is falling apart remember what's powerful inside of that is the sense of responsibility you can take on. You don't have to break down because things aren't working. You get to get up and say I know I can do something about this! I know that with everything inside of me I am meant to do my best and have faith that it will work out. Being a powerful woman means never wavering from your faith, never hesitating to give more than you expect in return, and becoming a "good finder." You can see the good in everyone, from within yourself, and in all circumstances – no matter how hard.

In fact, knowing you have something you're facing, something you have to deal with gives you the opportunity to share your power and grace with the people before and after you! You can share in the fact that you're only human and that you appreciate the guidance with which you've been given. You have the opportunity to be reminded of your faith and always feel held within the warm grasp of the word of God. In the words of Marianne Williamson, "We are all meant to shine, as children do. We were born to make manifest the glory of God that is within us. It's not just in some of us; it's in everyone. And as we let our own light shine, we unconsciously give other people permission to do the same."

So when you're done reading this, the choice is yours for how you will live your life. But I know who resides in you and the power you get to take on by being relentless in your love, your motivation, and your compassion for yourself and others. Imagine someone told you that a verse of scripture could help to give you the courage, motivation, and inspiration to overcome the obstacles in your life: Give her of the fruit of her hands; and let her own works praise her in the gates, 31:10-31. But what can you do by your hand that really makes a difference in your lives and those around you? You can be compassionate and generous! Simple! Here are a few easy ideas: try lending a hand to people who are less fortunate by volunteering in an animal shelter or soup kitchen. In fact, whatever you are dealing with in that moment of life will surely disappear against the adversity of those you help. Try planning ahead; a woman who thinks ahead can anticipate her needs and the needs of her family, her friends, and her significant other.

She opened her mouth with wisdom; and in her tongue is the law of kindness. Imagine how simply providing for someone else can also provide for you the strength and love to be unwavering! Imagine sharing your words of wisdom and affection.

But so many times the reason we feel stuck, demotivated, uninspired is because our world is centered on "me". So many times in our own lives, we're holding onto: "my rights, my time, my privacy, my peace of mind, my space." If we live egocentric lives now, we will reap the fruit of our own hands later.

Remember, you may have never considered these before; here are a few reasons why not:

1   Rejection. It's normal to reject this concept; to reject that image of a perfect woman, it's outdated and unrealistic. We're programmed by our culture to reject this depiction, even for many in the church.

But rejection comes through a real missing, a real piece of the puzzle that we have forgotten: You're not alone! Do you feel like you can't rise up? Do you wish you said all the right and perfect things and made the best decisions – but you didn't? It's OK! When you can't do what god asks by yourself –it's the starting place to victory! You're not a failure, you've just forgot who is really inside of you, God. He's there for you to lean on, trust, and have faith in. You can relax knowing that a life of faith can help you overcome anything!

2.   Acceptance. When you accept that someone else is there for you to guide you support you, and to stand up when you're not sure you can – everything becomes a possibility. You can get out of the cycle of struggle through acceptance.

There is still a very real place for gospel to apply to the challenges you may face in life and to find the strength to overcome it. For example, being a woman who is virtuous also means being a woman who can manage her resources. This is something you can easily incorporate into your life. But do you feel like you can't get through something: school problems, issues with your friends, poor grades, or even struggles with your parents? Remember that the inner power inside of you is very much alive! But also remember that you have people around you, resources! You have mentors, teachers, pastors, etc. who are available to help you manage your situation. And, if you are someone who looks to be of service to those around you it will always find its way back to you – especially in moments where you need it most. To sum it all up, give and you shall receive; you reap what you sow.

If something is falling apart remember what's powerful inside of that is the sense of responsibility you can take on. You don't have to break down because things aren't working. You get to get up and say I know I can do something about this! I know that with everything inside of me I am meant to do my best and have faith that it will work out. Being a powerful woman means never wavering from your faith, never hesitating to give more than you expect in return, and becoming a "good finder." You can see the good in everyone, from within yourself, and in all circumstances – no matter how hard.

In fact, knowing you have something you're facing, something you have to deal with gives you the opportunity to share your power and grace with the people before and after you! You can share in the fact that you're only human and that you appreciate the guidance with which you've been given. You have the opportunity to be reminded of your faith and always feel held within the warm grasp of the word of God. In the words of Marianne Williamson, "We are all meant to shine, as children do. We were born to make manifest the glory of God that is within us. It's not just in some of us; it's in everyone. And as we let our own light shine, we unconsciously give other people permission to do the same."

So when you're done reading this, the choice is yours for how you will live your life. But I know who resides in you and the power you get to take on by being relentless in your love, your motivation, and your compassion for yourself and others.

Renee Sunday

A Servant's Heart

A virtuous woman knows her purpose in life! This purpose is the foundation of her attitude and actions towards her husband and others. A virtuous woman is a help meet to her husband she is to help meet the needs of her mate. She will create an environment where her husband knows he never has worry about whether or not she is doing what is right towards him and others can trust her as well. The most important thing is to live one day at a time so that you do not get overwhelmed so that you can aware of who you are and what your mission is in life.

My husband is a Pastor and it is my goal and mission to make sure I do good by him, to think and do well by him, and to do the things he needs me to in order to help meet the needs of the household. I desire to actively serve my husband not because he is a Pastor or because I know he will do it in return, but because he is my husband and because of my love for him and God.

I remember the bible passage about Abigail and Nabal in 1 Samuel 18. See even though Nabal was surly and mean in his dealings Abigail did what she could to protect him she lived out the meaning of this scripture:

18 Abigail acted quickly. She took two hundred loaves of bread, two skins of wine, five dressed sheep, five seahs[b] of roasted grain, a hundred cakes of raisins and two hundred cakes of pressed figs, and loaded them on donkeys. 19 Then she told her servants, "Go on ahead; I'll follow you." But she did not tell her husband Nabal.

32 David said to Abigail, "Praise be to the Lord, the God of Israel, who has sent you today to meet me. 33 May you be blessed for your good judgment and for keeping me from bloodshed this day and from avenging myself with my own hands. 34 Otherwise, as surely as the Lord, the God of Israel, lives, who has kept me from harming you, if you had not come quickly to meet me, not one male belonging to Nabal would have been left alive by daybreak." 1 Samuel 25:18-44

Challenge:

Every marriage has tough times… I want to encourage you no matter how bad things may seem to do good by your husband and not evil and the Lord handle the rest. As the Proverbs 31 woman rose early in morning to seek the Lord you can do the same and he will give you direction on how to serve your husband and your household.

Prayer:

Lord, give a heart towards you and a heart to serve my husband and family. Help me not to see it as a burden, but as a blessing. Show me how to do my husband good and not evil all the days of my life. In Jesus Name ~ Amen

Krissti Bryant

Beauty is only skin deep

I grew up in church, but never had a real relationship with God until I was 19. When I was young (not that I am old now) I always thought my youthfulness and beauty would be what would draw the love I was looking for. Even though many times I looked at myself in the mirror I didn't even think I was pretty and found out quickly others thought the same. I was made fun on a daily basis, laughed at, pretty much mentally abused. If it wasn't about me being the oldest of seven and my parents getting busy it was because I usually wore clothes that were hand me downs.

I just wanted a friend I just wanted someone to love me and care about what I wanted. Well the older I got I found out that most often when guys liked me it was because they wanted one thing yes you guessed it to get between my legs. Those same guys who wanted that one thing are the same ones who would start rumors about me or try to date me while dating someone else. I was tired I kept looking for love in all the wrong places and kept coming up empty.

When I turned 18 years old I went to a Christian camp thinking I would escape it all I had never had sex and had never kissed a boy for that matter. I just wanted to get away of my parents to experience what I thought was life. I worked at this camp for a summer and quickly feel for what I thought was "Love". I was a worker in a kitchen and the boss over the kitchen challenged me to a competition and if I lost I would have to kiss him and guess what I accepted. After that day I thought I was in love my mom tried to warn me about him he was 10 years older than me I wouldn't listen.

After about a month or so I realized my mom was right. He started to tell me how stupid I was, he would tell how he punched through the wall in his mother's house, and he told me his mother promised him money if she would get married. He began to scare me to the point that one time he almost raped me. He got me alone in his cabin, which I wasn't supposed to in in the first place. I believe if I weren't there he would have assaulted me.

41

Not long after I tried to break it off with him and he pretty much threatened me and I was scared and decided not to, but then a month later I went to church and got some prayer and support and decided to break it off with him. He came to my job and once again tried to threaten me, but I decided this time I would not turn back I had God on my side I feared the Lord more then I feared him.

Not long after this I got a call from a private eye asking me if I knew this man "Mr. Steve W." and I said no and they said well you may know him as "Mr. Anthony M." They had told me he just raped a 16 year old and wanted me to testify. I was in shock I was grateful I felt bad for that girl, but I was glad for God's grace over my life it could have been me.

Proverbs 31:30 KJV

Charm is deceitful and beauty is passing, but a woman who fears the Lord, she shall be praised.

Challenge: I want to encourage you to know who you are in Christ and not to let others dictate to you who you are. When you look for the love that comes from the Lord he will bring that husband after God's heart. Lastly, Let your beauty flow from the inside out and most importantly fear the Lord.

Prayer: Lord, Please give me a love for you and an ear to hear what the spirit is saying. Help me to follow after you and to know who I am in Christ and at the right time bring that right Godly man into my life. ~ In Jesus Name.

Krissti Bryant

Burning the midnight oil

If anyone had told me while I was in my teens and twenties that I would be getting up before dawn to work, and furthermore, that I would be designing, baking, and decorating cakes for a living, I would have had a good hearty laugh with them! There are so many things wrong with that suggestion! Not only am I not an overly artistic person, but having been born into a fruit pie family, I don't eat cake. What's more, I certainly am NOT a morning person!! When I say I am not, nor have I ever been, a morning person, I mean it! On my own power, I do my best work in the wee hours of the morning, aka late night, and then go to bed and sleep until noon or later. Here is what I discovered about God, however. Not only does He have a grand sense of humor, but He also supplies us with every tool we need to fully become what He created us to be.

Shortly after my oldest daughter was born, I was invited to a friend's house to watch her pipe some decorations on a cake. I love learning about anything I have not encountered before, and agreed to go along and witness something new. Little did I know God was going to be birthing something new in me that would one day bless and support my family and many others. My daughter's first birthday came along and, not being able to afford a fancy cake on my own, I decided to try my hand for the first time at decorating one. The rest, as they say, is history. This creative thing I had never attempted before in my life came flowing out of my hands as if I had been doing it my entire life.

From that moment, I began to do more and more decorating, God gave me a growing passion and desire for this gift He had given me as well as an insatiable hunger to learn everything I could possibly learn. Before much time had passed, the cakes flowing from my hands were comparable to those seen on television, and a passion had been born. As I prayed about this new passion, God reminded me of the time I had dreamed of having a small old school bakery, but this time the dream was complete with fancy cakes. Over the next years, He grew and developed this dream. He refined His desire for me to ensure through the work of my hands, that not only

43

would my family have the additional financial support it needed, but also no person who was gifted with a cake He created through me would feel unloved or an orphan.

Today I am the owner of a bakery fully given over to my Lord Jesus Christ. He has gifted me with a business that allows me to be available for my family whenever needed. It allows me to bless others with the gifts He has miraculously instilled in me, and it has given me the opportunity to spread the good news of Jesus Christ in a gentle hands-on way. Today I am the owner of a bakery that requires me to rise from bed not only before the sun has risen, but sometimes after only one or two hours of sleep! Sound crazy? I have discovered when we step into the fullness of the purpose God has place upon our lives; He will also give all the tools. Would you believe me if I told you this bona-fide night owl rarely is tired during those before-sunrise mornings in the bakery? Most importantly, He has, through the anointing of my purpose In Him, helped me to bring order to my life.

My relationship with Jesus Christ comes first. If anything, ANYTHING comes before Him, life becomes chaos. The Bible says in I Corinthians 14:33, *"For God is not a God of disorder but of peace..."* Next in the order is my husband. Once again, if anything other than Jesus comes before my husband, our lives begin to unravel. *Ecclesiastes 4:12 "A person standing alone can be attacked and defeated, but two can stand back-to-back and conquer. Three are even better, for a triple-braided cord is not easily broken."* (Jesus, My husband, and I are a cord of three strands). And finally, my family... Everything I do, while fully for the glory of Jesus Christ, is for my family. This is the gift He has given me to support them.

"She gets up while it is still dark; she provides food for her family and portions for her servant girls." Proverbs 31:15

Challenge:

My challenge and encouragement to you is this: Place God first in all you do. Seek Him for your purpose, and do not be afraid if it seems entirely out of character. Do not balk at your purpose just because it may require something you never imagined you could do, like getting up before sunrise to begin the work of your hands. I promise you this: If you place Him first and foremost, if you honor your husband always as second in your life only to Jesus Christ, if you listen to the still, small voice of the Holy Spirit for God's call and purpose that is uniquely yours, you will never be without the tools, the energy, the blessing you need to carry that purpose and blessing out.

Alicia Hommon

A Woman's Worth

Where does your values and belief system originate? Who teaches you about self-esteem and self-worth? What happens if you never receive validation from those around you?

Well I can answer these any many other questions related to value. I grew up in a home unknowingly longing for the attention of my father who was the traditional provider who worked and made sure we had a roof over our heads. He stayed away from any emotional connection or intimacy during my childhood. My mom then overcompensated and showered me with love but she could not replace the love l longed to receive from my father. What happens to a girl who longs to hear I love you from their father? I turned to young boys to receive love and validation and attention.

I began to do things to receive attention and validation to feel good about myself the feeling never really lasted a long time but it gave me enough attention to want more. Even if the attention was negative it made me feel wanted and needed by a boy and later by a man. So I allowed these boys and men to shape my value and self-worth. Outwardly my self-esteem was strong but on the inside I felt lonely and tormented.

I remember the first time a boy touched me in the hallway. He rubbed up against my backside and outwardly I was offended but on the inside I loved the attention and the feeling. I thought he was attracted to me. I thought he wanted me, I thought that he saw me as pretty but the fact of the matter is that are value does not come from our earthly father, our friends or from boys or men. Are value comes from the lord.

Proverbs 30:10-31 describes all that God sees in us. Proverbs describes the characteristics of a noble woman. Compassion, wisdom and strong character are very important in the eyes of the lord and he esteems you as worthy if you exhibit these characteristics. Answers to the questions about what to do if you are never validated by another person in life just know that the Lord

46

validates you as worthy. Our answers must always come from the source. As girls and women we must consultant the one who created us the one who knows every want, desire and feeling that comes from within. Psalms 139:14, the voice translation read I will offer you my grateful heart, for I am your unique creation, filled with wonder and awe. You have approached even the smallest details with excellence; your works are wonderful; carry this knowledge deep within my soul. In essence God is so pleased with you and took some much time thinking about every detail of your existence. He wants the very best for you in every aspect of your life.

Challenge:

So I'm sure you are wondering what to do with this information or how to change if you struggle with some of the same things I did in the past. Here are few tips to help you continue to cultivate wholeness and worthiness in your life.

1. Find an accountability partner to share your thoughts and hold you accountable for the precious jewel that God created. Proverbs 31:10 a wife of noble character who can find? She is worth far more that rubies. The definition of ruby is a deep red, highly valued precious stone. God sees us more valuable than a ruby, however we must stand on his word, believe it and see ourselves as God sees us and hold others accountable to see us that way as well.

2. Set boundaries that honor how God views you. Don't allow others to devalue you. Say No, teach people how to treat you. If a friend, boy or girl treats you poorly you have a responsibility to tell them how you feel and expect a different treatment from them. If not, you have a responsibility to protect God's precious jewel by ending the relationship.

3. Apply the word to every situation. If someone devalues you go the bible and find out what God says about the situation or about you. You will find the answers you need to reject the negative comments made about you or find out all He wonderful things God has for you and wants to give you.

4. Find a positive circle of friends who support you and love. Remember you cannot live out all that God sees in you if you don't honor yourself.

"Other people's opinion of you does not have to become your reality"

Les Brown

~

"The way you treat yourself sets the standard for others"

Dr. Sonya Friedman

~

"Watch your thoughts, for they become words. Watch your words, for they become actions. Watch your actions, for they become habits. Watch your habits, for they become character. Watch your character, for it becomes your destiny."

Author Unknown

Latasha Matthews

Safe in His arms

When I was 18, I move to Cincinnati Ohio to be with my boyfriend I had from Grand Rapids Job Corps Center. I decided that after being on my own since 16 I didn't want to be at home anymore with my parents. On August 30th 1998, I boarded the bus at the Greyhound station and I moved out of state of Michigan. We stayed a few weeks with friends and finally got our own place. I really thought that I was in love when I left home to be with him. We didn't think of getting married so moving in together was the next option. We were both of two different religions; he was Muslim and I was a Christian. I knew in the back of my mind that we were not equally yoked because he didn't believe that Jesus was a son of God.

I still went ahead and continue the relationship anyway because I love him and I thought that I could convert him to becoming a Christian. When I moved to Cincinnati, I did find a church to attend. Sometimes I would go by myself to church on Sundays, but sometimes he would go with me. I must admit that I did see some red flags. He showed signs of physical abuse and mental abuse, but I ignored the signs and moved forward in the relationship. I felt sorry for him because he didn't have the best childhood and neither did I. I got pregnant the following year at the age of 19 and we both were very happy. What I didn't know was the relationship was about to head south real quick and take a turn for the worse.

In May of 2000, I had my first daughter. He was around during the first couple months after her birth, but he started to stay out late and leave me at home with the baby. He'd come in at all hours of the night and soon his cell phone was being hidden and people started calling. He was being a womanizer and I felt like I was stuck. My oldest daughter was less than six months old when I found out I was pregnant again.

In 2001, I gave birth again and again in 2002. His behavior had worsened, but no matter how much I went to church or prayed. He was indeed abusive in every way. He was cheating, lying, putting me down and doing any and everything to disrespect me. The relationship was over before he was removed physically. I had enough. In June of 2003, I ended the relationship and found a place to move. He moved in with another woman since he was no longer welcomed. I didn't care. I had to move on and get away from him. I knew I was going to be a single mom of three daughters, but I learned that I couldn't change a person and I should have waited on God, not fornicated and loved in sin and not been involved in a relationship that was not ordained by God.

I cried out to God and was challenged to step out on faith that He would take care of me, regardless of me not having enough money to move. I stepped out on faith and He made many doors open for me. In spite of fear and doubt, I trusted God to move on my behalf. He opened the door and I broke free and ran back into the arms of my Lord, my Savior.

Deliela Watkins

Overcomer

Life can be difficult, which is why it is so important to understand who you are and the purpose God has designed you for here on earth. When the world is storming around you and cataclysmic events are happening you can still find your joy, your hope for whatever lies ahead.

When I was a child I grew up in a household filled with violence, alcohol, everything was out of control. Every day I endured my father's verbal and physical abuse. I watched as he beat my siblings and my mother with word and whatever was closest to hit us with. I grew up being told I was worthless and that I would never amount to anything. You never really understand just how deep those words become rooted within your soul. I eventually began to believe everything he said, not feeling I had any purpose to even be here.

I began to shoplift when I was twelve eating bag after bag of candy to try and fill the space where my heart was broken. I just gave up on life. By the time I was fourteen I quit going to school, I would go out drinking at night and do whatever I wanted to. I became angry taking the rejection I felt inside and began to hurt anyone who tried to get close to me. I could not find joy anywhere or in anything. Even when someone tried to care I would just treat them as I had been treated. There is an old saying that hurting people hurt others and it's so true. My favorite words became "I don't need anybody."

The truth is I did, but I no longer believed in other people. I would lie in bed at night being afraid I would die not knowing where I would go. I took all of these feelings into my marriage and into my relationship with God not trusting not even knowing how to truly love anyone.

God has shown me what life without hope had done to my heart, to my husband and to my children. I came into a marriage angry, not trusting, feeling hurt and rejected. While it has been an ongoing process God has shown me how to forgive my father, family and yes even myself. I viewed my husband and my God the same way I viewed my father and it was only through God's love that I could

51

finally forgive and move forward. You see the more I looked back, the more I became anchored there not being able to move forward.

God can give you the faith you need to believe in Him, knowing that there will be good and bad times but, you will be able to find joy, rejoicing in every situation because of your confidence not in what you can do but in what your Father in heaven can do. He has already won the battle!

Isaiah 61:10

I will greatly rejoice in the Lord, my soul shall be joyful in my God; for He hath clothed me with the garments of salvation, he hath covered me with the robes of righteousness, as bridegroom decketh himself with ornament and as a bride adorneth herself with her jewels.

Challenge:

When you find yourself losing all hope and you feel ready to give up. Look up to your Father in heaven for help; you see He does His best work when we are in our weakest moments. As a woman of God, young or old you will face mountains in your marriage and family. However, if you look to God for your source of light, you will be able to rejoice through anything continuing to praise and worship as your life's story unfolds. You already know how this story is going to end that will be the source of your rejoicing.

Proverbs 31:25

Strength and honor are her clothing; and she shall rejoice in days to come…

Prayer:

Lord, please help me to hold on. I know that you are there, please help me to become that woman you called me to be living my life with purpose. Help me to rejoice even when I feel low. Give me the strength to face what today and tomorrow bring. Help me to become that wife, daughter, mother you have called me to be. In Jesus Name I thank you Amen!

Donna Rich

Through His Eyes

Self-esteem is defined as setting a high value on yourself. What you think you are that is what you are going to be. Proverbs 23:7 states, "As a man thinks so is he" - We must be mindful of how we think of ourselves. As a young woman growing up in this day we have to have a strong mind and honor ourselves daily. Young ladies we have got to know who we belong to. We are children of the Most High GOD and in His eyes we are beautiful regardless of shape, color, or irregularities. We must have a mindset that we are beautiful, intelligent, strong, and special.

I struggled with low self-esteem growing up. I always wanted to fit in and my feelings where hurt easily. I wanted everyone to be my friend and when they were not it damaged who I thought of myself to be. I was shy and withdrawn. I cried a lot and I struggled with fitting in. I was considered a nerd. I got good grades in school there is nothing wrong with that but worrying about what people think was the problem.

As I grew older in my teens and early adulthood I turned to food for comfort. Emotional eating is what they call it. I dated all the wrong guys just because I wanted to feel loved. I moved in with a guy and his mom in my early twenties just to feel loved and it was one bad relationship to another. This is what happens when you don't see yourself as a KING'S kid. Wrong thinking about you leads to wrong choices and bad decisions. GOD is the answer to all that we need. JESUS loves us regardless of what we do not love about ourselves.

Proverbs 31:25

Strength and honor are her clothing; She shall rejoice in time to come.

Challenge:

My challenge to you is to see yourself as GOD sees you. Ask GOD to give you confidence to be all that you are regardless of where you are in life. I guarantee you will be a true Proverbs 31 woman now and for your future. Your future is bright because GOD is already shining the light on your inner beauty directing you to fulfill the promise and destiny He has for you. Keep the faith and look unto JESUS who is the Author and Finisher of your faith. AMEN!

LaShanna Watkins

Be the difference

For such a long time I had always thought that my difference was a bad thing. I tried so hard to blend in but it never worked. I tried to hide who I really was, just to get others to like me and embrace me. As a result I never felt good enough, or beautiful enough, or intelligent enough in life. I was always comparing myself to others. I kept trying to align myself with the world's perception of beauty. Oddly enough, I never knew what that perception actually was. It's always changing! I thought my identity came from my makeup, or my clothing, or how I styled my hair. I wore so many masks that I had eventually came to almost losing myself. I had no clue what I liked, what I hated, and I had no idea what my calling was in life. I identified myself with others opinions of me.

That is until I cried out to the Lord to help me. I was drained. I was hurting. I had just had enough. It wasn't until I turned to the Lord that I became free. I didn't care about what the world or others had to say, I just wanted and hungered for God's truth in what He had to say.

Too often, we as ladies are so consumed in others opinions that we lose sight of God's truth about us. Even though we may be in this world, we are not of this world. We are daughters of the most High God. God has called us to be the light of the world and the salt of the earth. Our beauty is not in makeup, or in what we have or what we wear but in whom we are in God. What Proverbs 31:30 is saying is that charm alone is deceptive and beauty alone does not last, but when we choose to fear (trust and reverence) God and trust what He says about us, those are the women who will be greatly praised. You don't have to try and blend in with the crowd. And you don't have to be afraid of what other might say against you.

Choosing to fear God and not people.

Proverbs 31:30

Charm is deceptive, and beauty does not last; but a woman who fears the Lord will be greatly praised.

We are all created uniquely different and when we fully embrace who we are that's how the light in us will shine! So what exactly does God say about you? Here are just a few things…

1.) YOU ARE FEARFULLY AND WONDERFULLY MADE!

Psalm 139: 13-14 You made all the delicate, inner parts of my body and knit me together in my mother's womb. Thank you for making me so wonderfully complex! Your workmanship is marvelous- how well I know it.

2.) YOU ARE BEAUTIFUL!

Song Of Solomon 4:7 You are altogether beautiful, My Darling, beautiful in every way.

3.) YOU WERE PREDESTINED TO DO GOOD WORKS

Ephesians 2:10 For we are God's masterpiece. He has created us anew in Christ Jesus, so we can do the good things He planned for us long ago.

Challenge:

If you don't have one, I would encourage you to keep a journal. That way you can keep track of all the GOOD things God shows you and says to you. Take some time to yourself and write down all the things that make you, YOU! Ask the Lord to lead you to scriptures in the bible that reflect His heart about you. And when thoughts of doubt and fear try to enter in go over the thing God has said. In this you'll be building yourself up in God's strength and not your own.

Latrece Davis

Simply the Best

Self-worth seems to be a characteristic we are losing daily in our society. All you see are girls in videos wearing little to no clothes or the radios are playing songs about sexing this girl and sexing that boy. Whatever happened to songs that taught a guy to shower his woman with love? Or those that used to instruct a woman on how to cater to a hard-working man? Is the art of teaching through music and life lessons gone?

In the 31st chapter of Proverbs starting at the tenth verse, it begins to set the foundation of how a woman should conduct herself. It provides specific instructions for that of a Virtuous Woman. It is known that everyone will not fall under the category of a Virtuous Woman, but the second chapter of the book of Titus, verses two and three tells us how the older generation is to teach the younger generation. So with that being said, I must do my very best to instruct you, the next generation, how to be a young lady of self-worth. How am I going to do that? By walking you through this verse so you clearly understand who God has called you to be.

The KJV of Proverbs 31:10 asks the question this way:

>*"Who can find a virtuous woman? for her price is far above rubies."*

The NIV of Proverbs 31:10 says:

>*"A wife of noble character who can find? She is worth far more than rubies."*

The Amplified of Proverbs 31:10 says:

"A capable, intelligent, AND virtuous woman- who is he who can find her? She   is far above rubies or pearls."

The NLT of Proverbs 31:10 says:

"Who can find a virtuous and capable wife? She is more precious than rubies."

In each version of the verse, each one speaks to a value. This is not a dollar amount, but a moral and character amount. I truly like the Amplified version because it adds that you are intelligent and capable! Not only are you smart, but you can do above and beyond what you put your mind to! You don't have to settle for anything, for you deserve and can have the absolute best! As you respect yourself, your body, which is your temple, and your mind, others don't have a choice but to follow your lead. You that you don't have to act as everyone else acts. You are valuable and your value supersedes anything anyone else is doing that doesn't line up with respecting yourself.

Let me share my story with you. When most people look at and speak with me, they always feel I have had a good life. Let's not get it twisted, I haven't had a hard life that some have and still do, but it was by no means what I ever expected. Before I hit Kindergarten, the devil was trying to take me out. My brother picked me up from school and while driving home ran head on into a utility pole. They say I went flying towards the windshield and was badly bruised. I held the nickname of elephant man for quite some time.

Before I could officially hit middle school, my nephew's uncle tried to rape me… I was terrified, but I am glad I spoke up and they listened. After getting to high school, I was raped and impregnated at the age of 16. Still being young, I didn't know what to do besides abort them. I was a child that would have been forced to raise children I didn't willingly lay down to get. Part of me looks back and wonders, but it's done. All things happen for a reason…right??

I had my first child at 18 and a year later met the man who would turn out to be my abuser. He was smooth and FINE!! Light-skinned, buff, just oh la la… It's that right there that got me in trouble! Not truly looking into his character and morals. Sometimes it's necessary to stop and smell the roses of a man. I got pregnant immediately and by the time that baby was 6 months old, I experienced my first hit. I was driving down the road and said something slick and here comes his hand across my face. I almost hit oncoming traffic. It didn't stop there! I was almost stabbed in my spine TWICE!! I was told if I left him he would have me killed. I was isolated from friends and family, I was robbed by him... I remember one time he threw tea at me and I turned around and told him his momma raised a B**CH and then he slapped me and went outside to brag to the neighbor. I could go on and on, but I won't. Just know if I made it, so can you.

So as a victim of rape, domestic violence, low self-esteem, and much more, I want to encourage you to honor yourself! You don't have to have a boyfriend because everyone else does. You don't have to wear skimpy clothes because everyone else is. Most of all you don't have to have sex because everyone else is doing it. God calls you to protect your temple for it is precious. Look again at the scriptures. My daughter you are all that and a bag of chips!

I know you may be thinking how your friends are doing the things I am directing you not to do, but they are also reaping consequences you do not want to reap. This could be teenage pregnancy, teen dating violence, or even death. Not having self-worth costs more than having self-worth.

Challenge:

My daughter, my sister, my niece, my friend, you are worth so much more than that. You are worth the wait! You are worth the process to be chosen by the man God has for you. I ask you not to allow the pressures of this world to force you to conform to it, but you force it to conform to you. My queen, my princess you are worth all your heart's desires. Don't allow anyone to tell you differently! I love you and so does God!

Paula "Gods Elect Lady" Foster

Prayer is your call,
Intercession is your mantle...
Called to be a daughter in
Zion and raise you up to be an
example of brokenness,
righteousness, holiness
submissiveness...
Raising A Proverb 31
Woman

Virtuous Leader

One reward for having a love for reading was being promoted to fourth grade, from second. I enjoyed expressing words at an early age and tutored students as well. I never let my environment dictate what I could achieve, growing up in a poor community, I also wanted to make a difference in the lives of those who seemed to have lost their focus before they found it, for whatever reason. I became a teacher to identify, intervene and help at risk youth because I saw many children were not prepared academically for junior high and high school; I wanted to reach them before that point so they would not be discouraged. There were things in my own life that caused me to be withdrawn one of the effects were I was not as affirmative or confident it can be an intimidating time, unless you have a support system things can do downhill fast. When you don't get life lessons right you end up repeating them, don't set yourself up for this cycle. You have to know what you are there for and what you are not there for. You must also guard yourself from wanting to replace something or someone that is missing or lacking in your life, you can end up replacing a temporary issue with a worse more permanent issue, talk things over with someone you look up to before allowing your emotions, resentments and immaturity to act, get help not hell.

Staying focused now will affect the quality of your life in the future, being in control means not giving that power to anyone else. I quickly learned there is a price to be paid and a lesson to be learned when you do things out of Gods timing, sometimes it is a lifelong adjustment that has to be made, stop before you do something without regards to the consequences of your actions, I don't want your life to unproductive and filled with regrets so don't go down that path.

When things get stressful seek good counsel, pray for direction the reverence of God is the beginning of wisdom, giving in to pressure from your peers will get you into more trouble. Use your time wisely always have goals, completing them will motivate you to go farther. If you do fall no matter what get right back up, dust yourself off and finish. Don't allow ungodly influences to creep in, rather seek people who inspire, motivate and appreciate your uniqueness. Risky behavior is not something you can afford to be taking, one reason for this your brain is not fully matured at your age which affects your sense of reason and judgment, this is why your parents know best as you become more mature you will appreciate their guidance. Seek out opportunities that will allow you to perfect your field of study, if you ever need help do not be afraid to ask and don't worry about what people think, I have seen people refuse help because they were too proud, but they lost out at a crucial time when they could have been helped, don't be left behind it is your life be responsible and thankful for those who God has placed in your life. Stay close to your faith it is a guiding light in all areas of life and remember God will bless you for your obedience.

Lesson

As you read this verse and apply it to your life, look with your heart as well as your eyes, this is an intervention to encourage, strengthen and prepare you for the journey called life, watching over the affairs of *your Life,* now, will prepare you to be a good steward over them later as your responsibilities increase, having a good foundation to build on makes this much easier, be diligent in preparing for your education it all goes by so fast. The Proverbs 31:27 woman had her affairs in order, she knew what her children were doing at all times, watching out for their safety, making sure they completed their assignments, and behaving well. Throughout her life she was a role model as a young girl she learned many skills and trades as a woman those same skills served her well in the market place, do not let yourself become idle or be easily influenced, stay focused on your goals.

Challenge

Don't be a follower but seek to be around those who you can learn from, and don't allow anyone to have more authority and influence in your life than your parents do. Look at correction from your parents as a learning experience just as you would your teacher or other guardian they love you and know what is right for you, when they say they been there and done that you don't want to go there, please believe them. If they didn't provide correction they would not care or have your best interest in mind. The key to staying on the right track is knowing what you want to do, become or change, have a plan or goals set to achieve this, in addition to your school counselor do your own research, network and link with organizations that provide training and resources. Successful adults started by being successful students, it doesn't just happen or fall in your lap, don't expect another person to take care of you that is called co-dependence, your goal is to be self-sufficient. My hope and prayer is that you will challenge yourself to go beyond what is expected of you or how people see you and see yourself through Gods eyes. Your dreams can be as big as you want them to be, don't waste your gifts, develop and improve them through hard work and seeing your goals through to completion, whether that is to be a teacher, scientist, business woman, politician or social worker, you have the ability to create something unique and do it in excellence. Remove any limitations, doubts, past challenges, disappointments, anything not like God spoken to you.

Live your life like you are capable and in control, if you are not at the top of your class come as close to it as possible, never give up, be a role model for your generation, say "I am committed to being a life changer beginning with my own", you will then be on the road to success. You have the power to order your life and have an expected end, a blessed life full of opportunities, continue to honor your parents, uplift and motivate your siblings, families and friends. One of the traditions of the graduating class of Morehouse college was to say look to your left look to your right one of you won't be graduating, a motivated student spoke up and said, why not change this tradition and say, look to your left look to your right "You are Now looking at a Morehouse Graduate" I say to you Have Great Expectations Believe In Yourself You Are Worthy and UNIQUE!!!

Jeremiah 29:11   for I know the thoughts that I think toward you, said the Lord, thoughts of Peace, and not evil, to give you an expected end.

1 Corinthians 15:33   are not deceived: evil communication corrupt good manners Proverbs 3:6   In all thy ways acknowledge him, and he shall direct thy path

Psalms 1:1   Blessed is the man that walk not in the counsel of the ungodly, nor stand in the way of sinners, nor sits in the seat of the scornful.

Philippians 4:8   An idle mind is the devils workshop.

Sherry Turner

A Virtuous Perspective

It is completely possible to think that you have it all together one day and feel as though your life has completely fallen apart the next. It is completely real to be in a position today where you feel that your faith cannot possibly be challenged, but as soon as tomorrow faith seems to be a foreign word. What do you do when life as you know it is turned upside down, when you want to pray, but can only sit and stare? When the words that you once spoke so boldly have become silenced?

As I watched myself journey through life, had become quite proud of my natural accomplishments. I held a list of academic degrees and credentials, I was married to the first man that I had ever loved, and while we were not rich, every year was a progression, and my husband would actually remind me of the progression each year. Whenever I wanted to complain about what I did not have or what we were missing, my husband would always say " but, it gets better every year, right?", and of course it did, so I really did not have a reason to complain.

The early years of our marriage were not easy. We both worked for nearly nothing, and to top it off we had a baby girl to take care of. Sometimes not having enough money to buy her diapers, we would against what I had thought to be my "standards" buy the below the grocery store brand, or found ourselves having to add just a little more water to her baby formula than the directions called for . These standards of mine caused me to be embarrassed about the neighborhood and the apartment where we lived. While this was what we could afford at the time, I avoided inviting my friends over. I even avoided having my mother come to visit, and when they wanted to visit, I would arrange to meet them at different places in the city instead, so that they would not have to see where I lived.

During this time, I constantly reminded my husband that I was unhappy with where we lived, so in addition to his day job took on extra work at night and in the evenings to ensure that ends were being met, that we had food to eat, and that we could find a new place to live. One night while my husband was working nights, he came home to realize that my car had been stolen, from outside of our apartment, while our daughter and I were inside. Soon after that we made the decision to move from the neighborhood.

Our next move was seemingly better, at least initially. By this time, I had gotten a pay increase and had really started to become more career focused. Our baby girl was growing up, I had started back to school, and my husband continued with the extra work and it was all coming together. At least this is what we thought. One morning my husband came home late from work, when I saw him, blood was coming from his head. He seemed to be in a panic and rambling on about an accident, the car, and what had happened. He eventually calmed down enough to tell me that he had been in a car accident. He had apparently fallen asleep while leaving his job and hit a bridge. The passenger door was ripped from the car and he had evidently hit his head. I immediately took him to the emergency room with my then 3 year old daughter tagging along for the ride. Once we got there, he began to have an attack of some sort. The triage nurses had become concerned that he was having a heart attack. Fortunately, he was fine and was eventually released from the hospital.

After that day, he continued the night work for a while, however, I found myself in a constant state of fear that he would fall asleep while driving or that he would have an accident, so I asked him to retire from the night work. While the initial loss of income was noticeable, I decided to do something to help. To make up for the difference, I took on additional work that I could do from home. This increased our overall income and we again had an opportunity to move, but not before our apartment was ransacked, vandalized, and everything stolen. We were never able to find the culprits who had apparently broken into our apartment while we were away at work. Nevertheless, we were still able to see progress as we were approved for a home loan and moved into our first home shortly after the incident.

My work by this time seemed to be thriving. In fact the work that I had been doing from home had taken off tremendously. My home salary had become a near match to what I was earning on my full-time traditional job. My husband had by this time figured out a way to use his skills to earn additional income but not necessarily having to work late shifts. It all seemed to be going well, so we decided to have another baby. By the time my baby was due, I was earning more on my from home work than I was earning on my traditional job. I then decided that I would leave my traditional job and stay home. During my first few years of working from home, I earned well into the six figure salary, this seemed to be consistent for a while so, my husband and I decided first that I would get a new car, then another new, bigger house. We soon found the new car, then the new house, then another new car, and everything again appeared to be going well.

Then suddenly, there was a change in the way that my home and work handled business. I was told that changes had to be made and that I would not be able to obtain as much work as I had previously done. In the meantime, my husband became sick, needed surgery, and was no longer able to work the extra jobs. Suddenly within a year's time, we lost more than 70 percent of our income. Trying hard to maintain, we experienced situations that we thought were far behind us, including disconnected utilities, having to our children go without nice shoes and clothing, being unable to eat what we wanted when we wanted, losing everything from the furniture we sat on to the cars that we were driving.

My husband made his best efforts to encourage me through this situation. However, I was not listening. I felt that God had made promises to me that he did not keep. While I was not angry at God, I was disappointed. I had actually written down what I heard God promise to me, the time had come and gone and instead of promises being fulfilled, they appeared to have been denied. After this, I completely went into myself. I felt displaced because my family and I had to temporarily live with relatives in a loving, but unfamiliar environment in project housing. We had at least for the previous several years been seen as the ones who had it all together, family members and friends would come to us to borrow money or to help them out of difficult situations. They would use us as the example of the family members who had finally "made it", but it now seemed that the tables had turned and we were no longer the haves but the haves, but the have-nots. I remember reminding my husband of the statements that he made early in or marriage that "every year gets better". I felt that his statement was no longer true. It was not getting better, it had gotten worse. In fact, I felt that all of the years of hard work were useless and a waste of time.

I found myself sulking and complaining a lot, and my once positive, optimistic husband would have occasional bouts of pessimism and display feelings of despair. However, I was so involved with my own feelings that I became disengaged with my family. I did not attempt to encourage him when I noticed that he was beginning to sink into despair. Instead, I felt that this was how he should have been feeling, particularly since I felt that I had to suffer this setback unfairly. After securing a new place to live, I continued to sulk. I spent little time with my husband and children, although we were under the same roof. I felt that my image had been tarnished, my pride had been compromised, I was not living the life that I was supposed to live and I began to second guess those promises that I thought I heard God give to me.

Shortly after this, something happened that ended my pity party. Within a week's time, my husband, my son and myself had been involved in 2 separate car accidents. Each accident resulted in the vehicles that were a complete and total loss. The latter of the two accidents was an immediate awakening for me. On what seemed like a usually casual morning after dropping my daughter off at school, my husband somehow lost control of the vehicle. The car flipped twice. My son was somehow thrown from his car seat in the process and I remember seeing him flying above my head. I remember seeing my husband head hit the roof of the car as we flipped and the car landed upside down next to a sand bank. On the other side of the road were a creek and a bridge.

I remember yelling "Jesus" and calling for my son as I had assumed that he had flown out of the window. After the car had landed, I remember my husband's face as he panicked, asking me if I was okay, and asking me if I could see our son. At that time, neither of us could see our son. Those few seconds seemed like forever as we both began to call for him. My husband could not move his head because it was lodged at the roof of the car. I suddenly looked down as we remained upside down, and saw my son nestled near my feet. He was not saying a word, just nestled there silently in the fetal position.

After the accident, my first thought was about my daughter who had to be picked up from school by my brother-in-law. All I could think of is what would it have done to my daughter if my brother-in-law had to pick her up from school and inform her that her mother, or her mother, father, and little brother were no longer here. What was I leaving for my daughter? Did I want her to remember me as the person who always moped around the house and frowned at her father because she felt that her "image" was being compromised? Did I want her to see me as that disengaged mother who was so in to herself that she was not concerned about her father, her or her brother? Of course not, I wanted to be the example that she looked up to. I wanted be the person that she gave credit to for helping her to be a strong, fierce and well-developed woman someday.

My perspective totally changed after this. While my husband and I have always attempted business ventures together and have always discussed that we had a purpose that we would fulfilled together, we never dedicated ourselves completely to putting any of it into real action. After taking some time to reflect, we realized that one of the reasons why we never fully committed to God's purpose for us was because we tended to forget about His purpose for us and only thought about His promise to us when things were going good. We did not realize that when we were making the healthy six figure incomes that it was important to sow into our purpose. Instead we sowed into the houses, the cars, the vacations, the extra-curricular activities for the children, etc. While sowing into our children is also an investment and is in fact God's intention, our error was that we sowed into their activities before we sowed into our purpose and before we sowed into kingdom work. This backwards methodology of ours in essence produced nothing.

While we assumed that we were watering our promise, we were in actuality watering ground with the money that we made that did not have seeds planted in it. Watering ground with no seed, created mud instead of fruit. So there we were "stuck in the mud", spinning our wheels but unable to get out... the more we tried to get out, the more "stuck" we became.

The latter of the two car accidents symbolized for me that God had sent us a tow truck to get us "out of the mud". While the devil was hard at work to destroy us and to end our purpose prematurely, God, being the great opportunist that He is, used the car accident as an opportunity to open my eyes to His goodness, despite my personal feelings of "what I should have been or what I should have had". He used this as an opportunity to allow my husband and I to come together more intentionally and more aggressively for the purpose of following God's plan for our lives. This gave me the full understand of my role as my husband's wife and his helper. I truly understood in just those few seconds that it took for the accident to occur that it was not all about "my purpose", but that a piece of my purpose was to help my husband achieve his purpose.

As my husband and I continued to reflect, I realized that I had not been doing my part in helping him to be who God had called him to be. My moping and sulking often got him off track. My discontent with things such as where we were living, although it was truly what we could afford, caused him to make financial decisions that were not according to the timing of God. His wanting to please me leads him to agreeing to situations that were at times not prepared to become involved in. His striving to make me happy made him more apt to seek my direction prior to seeking direction from God. We soon realized the things we lost were actually not things that the devil had stolen from us, but were things that we had given to him. Yes. We gave to the devil. We gave him our cars, we gave him our homes, we nearly gave him our lives, all because we made poor decisions, decisions that we had not made through prayer. We sowed seeds in the wrong places and we reaped from where we had sowed.

Lesson:

Understanding that it is my husband's desire to make me happy, as it should be, I have a better perspective regarding what my role is in the process. My role is not to sulk and complain. My role is not to engulf myself in self-pity to get his attention in order to have my way. My role is to pray that God orders his steps. My role is to encourage him to fulfill his purpose. My role is to motivate him when he feeling low. My role is to assure him that I believe God with him for whatever the vision is that he has for the household that he leads. Knowing my role immediately propels him to his position. I am in his corner makes his desire to make the right decision even stronger than ever and give him the confidence to walk boldly into the authority that God has empowered him with.

My operating in my role has since made a tremendous difference in our lives. A sense of peace and harmony has consumed our family like never before. Restoration of what we lost is returning to us in a more miraculous and abundant fashion. We no longer dwell on those things that we gave to the devil, but we should press forward to fulfill the calling that God has on our lives and the purpose that he has for our household so that He can continue to honor the promises that He has in store for our family.

Proverbs 31:23

Her husband is respected at the city gate, where he takes his seat among the elders of the land.

Challenge:

Spend the next 14 days complimenting your husband. Commit to no complaining, no pouting, no doubting of the decisions that he makes for the household. When you pray with him each night, ask God to order his steps. Ask God to teach you how to fulfill the piece of your purpose that enables you to help your husband to fulfill his purpose. Do this so that your husband can hear you say it.

Tykeysha Boone

No More Walls

Hello ladies! I want to share with you what the Lord showed me throughout the years about putting up walls. Many people, including myself, have put up walls due to past hurts, rejection and low self-esteem. For me, it was all of the above. As a younger lady I never saw myself as being beautiful because I was told by people that I wasn't because I was overweight, have a gap in my teeth and wore glasses. I always believed that that was true because I always based my value on what other people thought about me and never on what God said about me. And I want you to understand how what God says about you can help avoid putting up walls.

Let me first explain why I chose Proverbs 31:30. Okay, as I said in the above paragraph I always based my value on beauty, but what does the first part of the scripture say? "Charm can be deceptive and beauty doesn't last…" If you base your value on vain things you'll just wind up getting yourself hurt over and over again. This will lead to depression which will cause you to put up walls. But how do you know your value and how do you know what God says about you? By spending time with God. This is where you're true beauty flow from.

1 Peter 3:3-4

"Your beauty should not come from outward adornment, such as elaborate hairstyles and the wearing of gold jewelry or fine clothes. Rather, it should be that of your inner self, the unfading beauty of a gentle and quiet spirit, which is of great worth in God's sight."

This doesn't mean that you can dress nice and whatnot, just don't base your beauty on it. I remember when I was in school and I saw so many girls with boyfriends and I never had one. This made me feel really insecure because I thought that I wasn't pretty enough to have a boyfriend. So when guy finally started to ask me out, I would put up walls and be really rude to them and sometimes I was just rude to people, period. If I did tell them yes I would be with them, I would always try to avoid getting too close. This also prevented me from getting close to family and my friends. People would always tell me that I was shy because of that but really it was fear of rejection. See, that's what the enemy wants you to do. He wants you to think less of yourself because He doesn't what you to do what God have called you to do.

Proverbs 3:6

"In all your ways submit to Him, and He will make your paths straight." (NIV)

After I had realized what the enemy was trying to do, I decided to give back to God. I had the hardest time looking people in the face when having conversations with them, I always walked around with my head down and when it came time for me to get a job, I've always said I wanted a job in something where I didn't have to deal with much people. The Devil really had me in a bind and I felt like I could get loose. Until the Lord showed me one day that He wanted more of me. He wanted me to hand everything over to Him. No more do I listen to what the world thinks about me I believe what God said and says about me. As I started spending more time in worship and reading the bible, the Lord started to show me who I really am and what things I really liked. I had to stop being a people pleaser so people won't see that I had walls up and start pleasing God. Once I started to please God and started doing what He told me to do instead of what people said I should do, I started getting more confidence and boldness started to arise in me. And I know it wasn't me because the Lord had me doing things that I would never had done. It was hard at first but once I put away self and let God take control it was easier because I knew it wasn't of my own words.

Allow God to work on you because He wants to show you so many things about yourself that you didn't know about yourself. Think about it, if you're putting up walls so that people can't get in because of your "insecurities", you're not allowing God in. This will lead you down a rough path that will lead to depression. God does not want you in that position at all. He wants to love on you but you have to be willing to let Him in. I know it might be hard at this young age because of the peer pressure but you have to stand out. Remember that you are the salt of the earth meaning you're the one that brings flavor (the difference). People are always looking for something different in a person, that's why we have all of these fads that fade very quickly. But guess what? Jesus isn't a fad and He will never fade. So that mean neither will your salt if you continue in His presence. It's time to tear down those walls of because of past and even present hurts and allow God to heal your heart. There is so much freedom in following Christ instead of following the world.

1 John 4:7-8

"Dear friends, let us practice loving each other, for love comes from God and those who are loving and kind show that they are the children of God, and that they are getting to know Him better. But if a person isn't loving and kind, it shows that he doesn't know God-for God is love."

The main thing that needs to be done is forgiveness. Your heart can't be healed because of un-forgiveness. No matter what the person may have done to you, you still have to forgive. Love is the most important commandment that we have. If we don't walk in love, we aren't being obedient to God. And harboring un-forgiveness will cause you to put up walls because you don't want to be hurt again. It used to be hard for me to let things go but once I realized that we're not fighting against flesh and blood but against the spiritual world, it made it easier to let things go and give it to God. Sometimes the Lord still has to remind me that that's the case and not take it to heart.

So my challenge for you is when you spend time with God, ask Him to show you what walls you have built up and to show you who you really are. Listen for His voice at all times because He is the only One that knows what you have been through and where you are going. He knows you more that you know yourself.

Proverbs 31: 30

"Charm can be deceptive and beauty doesn't last, but a woman who fears and reverences God shall be greatly praised." (LT)

Tymithia Davis

Struggle No More

I was a lost little girl, with no direction in life that I can recall. I was an unwed mother at the age of 16, just living life with no plan; and looking for love in all the wrong places. At the age of twenty one I gave my life to Christ, and found hope, true love and purpose. I now share my life with other young women to offer them hope; helping them to plan their lives and fulfill their God-given purpose. – Jacqueline Barnes

A Proverbs 31 woman knows the source of her strength; so she starts her day in the presence of her Lord; quiet intimate time with her Creator. This sets the day giving her the spiritual strength, joy and peace to guide her through the day.

She makes time to learn and grow through educating herself; learning about the world, increasing her skills, and helping others. She understands that she only has one body and she honors it by feeding her body the right foods that will build it up. She gets proper rest, replenishes her body with clean fresh water and strengthens her body with exercise. She's not trying to imitate anyone else because she knows that she is uniquely created and looks only to maintain a healthy lifestyle with a healthy weight specific to her unique body type. She knows that being physically fit helps her to have energy and strength to handle her busy lifestyle.

She is ready for the day; she is strong spiritually, strong mentally and physically fit. She is not afraid of hard work. This chic is the total package. She is the Proverbs 31 woman.

Proverbs 31:17 (TAB)

She girds herself with strength [spiritual, mental, physical fitness for her God given task] and makes her arms strong and firm.

Challenge:

We all struggle at one time or another with our weight, establishing healthy eating habits, making time to work out, reading our bibles, spending time in prayer, studying for school or homework and taking care of the house (keeping our rooms clean, etc.).

To take the struggle out of it, we have to find out what works for us personally: I don't have to look like girl in the magazine or on television; I have to learn to be healthy and physically fit for my body type. I can admire others but I create my own style. Choose one thing you can start doing today:

-Walk 30 minutes a day

-Get 8 hours of sleep

-Drink 8 glasses of water a day

I don't have to spend hours in prayer; maybe I can spend 5-10 minutes starting my day off talking to God, and then talk to Him all through the day. I can memorize a scripture and meditate on it throughout the day. That way I'm hiding God's word in my heart. Choose one thing you can start doing today:

-Spend 10 minutes talking to God

-Memorize Scripture once a week

I want to be successful so I study and complete all my homework assignments. I'm not afraid to ask for help from a teacher, a tutor or an adult when I need it. Choose one thing you can start doing today:

-Create a specific time for studying and completing homework

-Ask for a tutor in a subject I'm struggling with

-Reduce TV and Social Media time

-Read a new book every week

To make things easier around the house, I can do my part by keeping my room clean (which helps me to think clearly and sleep better without the clutter) and I can help with other chores when needed. Choose one thing you can start doing today:

-Set a certain day to clean/organize my room every week

-Volunteer to help with additional chores

Jaqueline Barnes

Preparing for THE Husband of God's Choice

&

Loving Yourself in the Process!

Preparing for a husband takes much prayer, great submission and a mighty will. That, in itself, was a very hard lesson for me to learn. I knew that I wanted to someday get married and live happily ever after. I actually thought, as a child, I knew who that person was going to be. That part was just a fantasy and so life went on.

As a young person growing up in an era where you had to dress or look a certain way to fit in, I was always picked on because I didn't look or dresses like everyone else and sometimes it were just because. I never considered myself a pretty or attractive person. I always thought that my skirt had to be 3 inches above my knee or my pants so tight that I couldn't breathe to even get noticed by a boy. Even though I never dressed that way, that is how us girls back then, were categorized. Of course the boys liked it because the girls dressed to reveal instead of dressing to appeal. This revealed everything that the guys were and still are curious about...the woman's' body. There is no respect in prematurely revealing what God, from the beginning, meant to stay covered. A lot of young ladies today do not understand that they do not have to be revealing with their bodies to be noticed. A person is noticed by how they represent themselves. We have to remember that we are women of God and women of purpose and that He only wants what is best for us. We, as women, are designed to be a help meet, not a door mat. We, as women, are designed to be loved and cherished, not beaten and destroyed. Therefore, we must seek God diligently and be willing to hear from Him and trust His will for our life.

Throughout my teenage years, I begin to see that God wanted so much more for me, I just had to accept it. Well, I knew better, I just was not ready. Being the only girl left at home after my brother and sister went to college, made things a little more difficult for me. I was always in the limelight or should I say under the radar. My mother kept me in church as well as bible study to ensure that I was getting fed spiritually, but what I loved the most is that she always prayed for me. Even now, she still prays for me. Don't get me wrong, I have made plenty of mistakes in my life and all I can say to that is BUT GOD! Having a parent that constantly prays for me is the best blessing I could ever ask for and appreciate. I can truly say that I am here today because of my mothers' prayers and the grace of God.

Reflecting on my first marriage, I was so excited. I wanted so badly to be married. A couple of days prior to the wedding, I can remember standing in front of my bedroom mirror at my mothers' house holding my wedding dress up against me. I started praying and asking God if I were to do this right now. God's answer to me was clear and straight forward – "No!". My response was "Ok, God" and continued to prepare for my wedding the following day. I *completely* ignored the voice of God and His will for my life. Needless to say that, in doing what I wanted to do, I was hit with a lot of challenges that I really did not have to face had I been obedient to God's will. *(Proverbs 3:5-6)* I thought that I was ready to be a wife at that point in my life, but I found out the hard way that I had to be happy with myself first before I could ever make another person happy. Spiritually and emotionally I was broken and did not realize it. I needed to heal from past heartaches, insecurities, disappointments, uncertainties, the feeling of neglect and failures that I had experienced in my life up to that point. I was torn between where I was and where I knew I should have been which was fully in the will of God and allowing Him to lead as I follow. Even though that marriage was very short lived, I learned from it and I prayed through it.

Regardless of the circumstance or situation, we are to always seek God first before we make a decision about anything. If His answer is No, trust that He has a reason for telling you No for right now and seek the revelation. *(Matthew 6:33)*

Lisa A. Johnson

I am a Proverbs 31 Woman!

Oh the joys of being a woman, a daughter, a sister, a niece, and A WIFE .We wear many hats, so many hats we forget that God made us this way. However when we were born, God knitted us specifically and uniquely to one day become A WIFE. Growing up I saw for myself what a husband and wife looked like together in the same house which were my parents. I can't say it was always peaches and cream for them, however they made it last 48 years later. When God sends you the "One" he picked out for you, you will know it. It won't be the man you fantasied about, saw on TV or in a movie, or a magazine, not even a perfect man, however it will be a "God's specialty "made just for you.

When I met my husband, it was at our church that we grew up in about 14 years ago. Little did I know that he was there the whole time and I didn't even know it? Wow, see how God sets things up? Before we would meet, I had to get myself together first. At that time I was in school and I was just getting out of a relationship. I had some issues especially in school with being a slacker. In other words I didn't have a drive. Although my parents taught and instilled values in me, I started realizing that I had to WAKE UP and smell the coffee on my own! If I wanted this and that and to become whatever I desired to be in life I had to pick up the pace. I had to do what Proverbs 3:5-6 says "Trust the Lord with all my heart, and don't depend on my own understanding. Remember the Lord in all I do, and he will give me success". Ladies, I had to do it with my WHOLE heart.

The previous relationship I was in prior to meeting my soon to be husband was not healthy, in fact I believe the lack of perseverance from him rubbed off on me some. Let me tell you, be very cautious of what type of crowd you hang around. Are they dreamers, doers, optimistic, history makers or fire starters? Or are they doubters, pessimist, or finger pointers that you are associating with? Proverbs 13:20 says " Become wise by walking with the wise; hang out with fools and watch your life fall to pieces".

I met my husband at a time in my life, where I was hanging with the wrong crowd! Little did I know that he would be the one to help put the pep back in my step (smile)! We met on a Sunday and that is usually when we would see each other at church service. Actually I didn't notice him, he noticed me. In fact, every Sunday he spoke to me after Sunday school .In my mind I'm like "Why is this man always speaking to me and going out his way despite the crowd to talk to me? Well those greetings from him turned into lovely conversations. I began to look forward to talking to him, and when he wasn't there I was a little disappointed! Those conversations turned into phone calls which later turned into dates.

We talked about our dreams, our aspirations, or accomplishments and things we had in common, things we wanted to do different if we could. There were a lot of things we had in common, which was very surprising to me. What I loved about him was that he was always encouraging me and pushing me. It is so nice to have someone in your corner to encourage you, especially when you think you can't encourage yourself!

You know I was raised in a Christian home and my parents instilled the biblical principles, and values inside me, and I love them dearly for that; however I needed a push a lot of times when it came to everyday life and facing the world. Little did I know that God was creating someone to do just that! My prince and I dated for about a year and it was like a new adventure for us. Now let me tell you, I was a shy and quiet young lady, and he was the opposite, but in a good way (smile). He helped bring out the confidence in me. There is a Turkish proverb that says "A lion sleeps in the heart of every brave man," which I thank him for helping bring out the lion in me (smile). When a man and women uplifts each other and it's not just one sided while starting from being just friends, to dating, then marriage, it's a beautiful thing. Just knowing that he has your back and he knows you have his back makes him grin from ear to ear (smile).

I think about Lalah Hathaway's latest song "Something". Some of the words resonates in my mind, and it says "You and I have something in common, oh how I long to be around you, it's been a revelation, you've been an inspiration to me ".When God sends your mate to you, it will be something very special. Don't allow the world to tell you that your "biological clock is ticking" and you need to be married at a young age or you will dry up and rot. Don't allow them to tell you, "you can do it ALL on your own" without a man. Genesis 2:18 says *"Then the Lord God said, "It is not good for the man to be alone. I will make a helper who is right for him."* Allow God to lead and guide your steps, and don't allow fear to enter in, continue to feed your faith with God's Word in all areas of your life.

Proverbs 31:11

Her husband entrusts his heart to her, and with her he will have all he needs.

Challenge:

Becoming a wife is beautiful; however it takes work to keep your marriage beautiful. Once you become that woman for him, love him, honor him, encourage him, have his back constantly and you will be forever in his heart! Ladies I challenge you to respect yourself, your body, and others. Don't allow the enemy to enter your mind and your heart to become bitter because it hasn't happened yet. You become better instead. *Proverbs 4:23 says "Guard your heart above all else, for it determines the course of your life."* Ladies you are worth waiting for! Let God start his good work in you to become that Proverbs 31 woman God created you to be!

Aisha Z. Adams

Transition—Discovering Self Worth

"And God said, "Let us make man in our image, after our likeness: and let them have dominion over the fish of the sea, and over the fowl of the air, and over the cattle, and over all the earth, and over every creeping thing that creepeth upon the earth." Genesis 1:26

"I will praise thee; for I am fearfully and wonderfully made: marvelous are thy works; and that my soul knoweth right well."
Psalm 139:14

WORTHLESS UNLOVED UNFORGIVEN DIRTY UNINTELLIGENT USELESS.

These were just some of the things that I felt about myself. No one ever knew it because I had a smile that was brighter than the sun and knew what to say, when to say it, and how to say it. I wore a mask every day and I never wanted anyone to see through the mask. I was afraid. Afraid that no one would love or could love the real me; the real me that I needed so desperately to hide. I was shattered, broken, and damaged—damaged goods walking around in a body pretending to be free. I was bound and no one could save me. I was perfect in every way and had everything going for myself and no one knew just how hurt I was. I needed help and would not let anyone close enough to truly help me. The worst part was I didn't even know why I was hurting or what had made me feel this way. When had it all begun and who were the principle players in this game that I called my life? Would the maze ever end or would I carry it with me to the grave? There was no use in believing in myself because I was nothing to believe in. I was hopeless and certainly not the princess that everyone thought I was. I did not deserve the pedestal that I was put on day in and day out. Soon I would fall and there would be no one there to catch me. I was on the verge of breaking. Who would be there to put the pieces back together again?

Have you ever felt this way? Have you ever stepped outside of yourself only to look at your life spinning out of control and it seems that everyone believes in you more than you believe in yourself. They know the phony and you know the real you, right? Isn't this a lonely place to be? You're in a dark cave and there is no light at the end of the tunnel, or so you think. Listen carefully as we take a journey from insecurities to inner security…from hurting to healing…from self-defeat and condemnation to self-worth and restoration. God wants to restore you as you take this journey with me so open your heart and soon His healing touch will set you free. As you listen to the Lord while reading further, I'd like to open my heart to you that you might feel a touch of God's love and peace the same way He gave it to me. Who really knows when we start to feel unworthy and unloved? I don't really know where my pain began yet I do know that one day I woke up feeling like my life was not what I wanted nor was it what I had envisioned it would be. I had to take self-inventory because I was broken and I was hurting and had no idea why. I began to look at the events of my life and I discovered a pattern.

When I was about 10 years old I was mildly sexually abused— fondled. What had I done to deserve this? Why was I chosen for this act and why wasn't I protected against it? Had I been such a terrible person that this was my punishment? This was someone that I trusted, so does this now mean that I cannot trust the men in my life to treat me with respect? I was hurt more emotionally and mentally than physically and I did not know how to turn the tape recorder of my mind off.

As I got older I really did not have many friends. I chose to spend more time with my family and on my studies and my choice to do this gave the impression that I thought I was better than other people. Then I started being featured in the newspaper on a regular basis for various activities. This didn't help my situation. I desperately wanted real friends who would care about me for me and not for what they thought I could give them.

I wanted to date and feel the affection of a young man yet I did not date until I was 18 and in every relationship (there were only a few) I was either cheated on or he chose his friends over me. I was never a priority. Some even abused me emotionally or took advantage of my kindness, including my finances. Was I wearing a sign around my neck that said, "I am weak, vulnerable, and devoid of feeling, please come and take advantage of me?" I tried to buy love and acceptance from friends and men because I had developed a notion that I could not be loved just for who I was. I was fat, ugly, and had nothing to offer to anyone. I knew I had gifts and talents yet I did not use them the way others thought that I should so I was rebuked for that too. Everything in my life said I was unworthy and the brokenness continued.

Until the Lord said enough is enough. As the Lord began to show me the events of my life through His eyes I began to see a different picture. God removed the shingles from my eyes so that I could see clearly! I realized that it was not my fault that someone else had a problem that they decided to take out on me by abusing me. I began to see that concentrating on my studies and spending valuable time with my family helped to mold my character and make me a stable person who enjoyed learning and therefore had a lot to share. I found out from a neighbor who liked me that my brother, who is 3 years older than me, had sent the word out that if anyone tried to date me or even look in my direction they would have to deal with him! He told everyone that I was off limits and he would come back from the army just to defend my honor. I wasn't ugly at all, there were plenty of people who wanted to date me but it wasn't worth having to deal with my brothers (I had three and I was the baby and only girl!). It wasn't my fault that my boyfriends and estranged husband didn't love and respect me enough to remain faithful. Their infidelity was proof that they didn't even love and respect themselves. The bottom line, I could not control the actions of others—I am not responsible for them. I can only control Kelley and I am responsible for myself. I am accountable to God.

Then God began to tell me how He saw me. He told me that I was created in His likeness and image and He doesn't make any junk. He let me know that I am fearfully and wonderfully made and that everything was made to give Him Glory. That makes me feel better because I know that when I look in the mirror I am looking at a piece of Heaven. I was made with God's hands and He knew me before I was ever conceived in my mother's womb. He made me the way that I am so who is man to say that I am no good and who am I to trust man's opinion of me more than I trust God's. God began to show me how I had allowed other people's insecurities about themselves to penetrate me and to help determine how I felt about myself. The biggest thing that God showed me is that I belong to Him and I AM the righteousness of God. He loves me so much that He sent His only Son to save my soul. Jesus paid the price for me and God let me know that I was so precious that He sent His son just for me. He burned this fact on my heart so that anytime I begin to feel unworthy I can look to my heart and see His Son hanging on the cross just for me. The best part is that He rose from the grave and is now resurrected in me. God showed me who I am and who He has designed me to be. It doesn't mean that I became perfect; it just means that I stepped forward and became comfortable with me. Some people still don't like or understand me and that's ok. That's their problem, not mine. I am not living for their approval because God is the Lord of my life and the approval I seek is His. I can hold my head up high and know that as I humble myself to God and submit to His will that He will lead me and guide me in the path that I should take. God is the center of my joy and the head of my life! What He has given to me the world cannot take away.

The greatest gift He gave me was His Son and then came the gift of loving myself. I am not a dumping ground for anyone and I will not settle for the things of this world. My self-worth has skyrocketed because I received the Word that God has for me. I love myself and I love the Lord. I thank Him for my trials because I can use them today to help you and many others to receive His love and to reject the world and its opinions of you. The devil thought he had me and Jesus said NO! I am His and He is mine and I can walk forward in my life in the peace and love that only God can give.

I have transitioned! The chains have been broken and I am FREE to love me and to be ALL that God has created and called me to be. Let God set you free. Let Him use you so that you can move forward and use your life as a testimony to help others. Before the testimony there is a test! With God's love and guidance I passed mine. Let God be your study buddy and you'll pass yours too. Your Report card will show the only grade that matters...FREEDOM IN CHRIST!

Take some time right now to make a list of the things that you are critical about in yourself. Now make a list of the wonderful things about yourself. Compare the lists and I am sure the list of positive and wonderful things outweighs the negative list. Talk to God about those negative things that you feel and remember your tongue has power. As you submit the negative list to God, He will begin to show you how to have more confidence in Him. Begin to study the positive things. You can use post it notes around the house, you can write in your journal, or any number of things. It's so easy to remember the negative stuff and this exercise will help you to focus on the positive. You are made in God's likeness and image. You are beautiful because of Him!

Minister Kelley Sawyer

Who is a Proverbs 31 Woman?

He that finds her finds a good one indeed.

Trustworthy, strong and smart.

She takes care of BUSINESS!

Who is a Proverbs 31 Woman?

Works hard – Yep.

A good cook – You know it!

Can save a coin - Definitely!

Who is a Proverbs 31 Woman?

Crowned with nobility as she glides through the trials of life.

Courageous in scarlet and majestic in purple like in the Good Book.

She makes him proud!

Who is a Proverbs 31 Woman?

My grandmother - that's who.

My grandmother is the nurturer of the family. Although she had my mother out of wedlock and later become a divorcee with a son to raise, she somehow landed on her feet and kept her stuff together. What that meant to me was that she was of sound mind and body, worked every day, had her own place, and took care of the business of life. She always had something to read in her home, from Essence and Jet Magazine to National Geographic. She was the only person knew with an entire set of the Encyclopedias!

Back in the old neighborhood the oasis that was my grandmother's home was very important to me. It seemed she had everything in that small two-bedroom project apartment. It was always clean, chaos free, and a place where I could have all the food I could eat. I can remember a couple of times just crouching down next to the gate on her door waiting for her to come home from work. Unlike my mother she always came home. Once inside I could count on Pinwheel cookies and milk, good meals and good treatment, rather than where I was escaping from, which was usually some relatives that my mother dumped us off with, who often grew tired of us and treated us like a nuisance at best and cruelly at worst. Not so in apt. #203. "Bunch" as folks called my grandmother, short for Honey Bunch, because she was so sweet, showed me what it was to be a real woman; a Proverbs 31 kind of woman. She was your quintessential strong black woman. She had her stuff together and never counted on anyone to help her; she allowed me to stay as long as I wanted. However long or short, I enjoyed my time with my grandmother to the utmost. She made me feel safe.*

Who is a Proverbs 31 Woman?

Thanks to my grandmother, I am!

And you?

Lessons:

> Be brave.

> Be persistent.

> Be loving and compassionate.

Challenge:

Identify situations that you will demonstrate bravery and persistence. Pinpoint individuals that you will show more love and compassion.

Yvette Pye

Briar Patch

My first memory is one that I have wondered is it a memory or a dream to handle how I felt or view something. This memory or dream is that of being thrown down a flight of stairs as an infant and my grandmother catching me in a laundry basket, because, she just happens to be walking by at the time. I am left to wonder exactly what it is, a memory or a dream. Is it real or was this just the way my young mind handle being left in the care of my mother's mother, my grandmother while she continually would take my younger brother with her to live? My mind just wonders.   Now, for my next memory, the first part of this flash that plays through my mind is a great one. It is me as a young girl riding on the shoulders of my natural father as he walks towards the amusement area of Ocean City. But, the other half of this flash is not one that is so pretty. It is me hearing my father say to me "come lay down with me" and then him taking off my pants and my underwear and saying "I want to show you that I love you". This was the very first time my father or any man had every raped me. I guess you may say raped that is the wrong word is it not? No, it is not because there was actual intercourse/penetration; therefore it was rape and not molestation. Molestation is just the fondly, touching, and or showing for a sexual gratification, where with rape it is the actual sexual act for gratification. This is the first memory of a four year old of her now jailed father. This violation caused such physical and mental pain, not to mention the total confusion of it all.

From this point in my life it seems like it has been one thing after another, bad things after bad things. To me it seemed as if there was never a time to heal or recovery from any of the things that was happing to me. My life seemed to be full of hurt and pain. My life seemed to be one where the moment I took a "half" a step forward I was knocked 10 steps back.

I know you may say it could not have been that bad and perhaps your situation may even be worst. Just before you decide to fully think that through let me give you a short list of just my childhood. My mother was very abusive in the way of it being physical, verbal

94

and mental. Don't get me wrong I was not the perfect child, but I was a child with a lot of issues and no one to help or explain any of it, therefore I needed an outlet. My grandmother was not much different than my mother but, I did feel that she loved me because at least she kept me around. She was just as physically, verbally and mentally abusive as my mother. Hey, my mother had to learn it from somewhere.

Let's not forget the extreme bullying and picking on at schools and younger and older family members. I say schools, because, for two years I would live and go to school with my grandmother and then for one school year I would be with my mother. Trust, as soon as the school year was up I and my younger brother would be sent to live with my grandmother for the summer. The only difference would be is at the end of the summer my younger brother would leave and go back to live with my mother and I was left behind.

Next on this list is that I was forced to go to my grandmother's sister house (my Aunt) from time to time where her husband, my uncle, raped me. Only to leave there and go to my father's relative house to be raped by my cousin by way of convincement, to only leave there to be molested and raped by a family friend. Now, was this all in the same day by no means no, but you do get my drift. Last, but not least, only to get to 12 years old and be forced to go live with the very father who raped me at four and a few other times in between and his new family (his wife and my younger half siblings).

Yes, I can go on about the hurt and the pain of my childhood, my young adult life or even my adult life, but why. I am now almost 43 years old, the older to four younger siblings and a mother of two young men, but I am tired of being stuck. I no longer want to carry my yesterdays into my todays, because, it will keep me from my tomorrows.

You may ask why she would call this "Briar Patch". Well the "Briar Patch" is my lesson. God speaks to Paul in 2 Corinthians 12:7-10 about the thorn in his side that he (Paul) had asked God to remove and God being God basically said NO. He was not going to remove it but, let it remain and he basically just needed to deal with it. (This is just how I view this story). But, sometimes life ends up giving you thorns (life happenings) and you therefore live your life in a "Briar Patch" always been reminded of all those thorns (life happenings) that you have been left to live with.

As I thought about the fact that this is my life, I am left to think about Proverbs 31:17 and more on the scripture mention before. Just because I live here in this "Briar Patch" it has strengthen me to reach out to someone else. It helps me not to be so judgmental, it has given me the gifts of mercy and compassion, and it has made me to be a protective, loving and different parent. Therefore, I am getting to the point where I am not allowing these thorns to hinder me and remembering that His grace is sufficient for all that has come to past, that which is happening now and that which is yet to come. I have come to hear God say "if I have created the rabbit to live and survive in the "Briar Patch" then why can't I do the same for you.

Proverbs 31:17

She sets about her work vigorously; her arms are strong for her tasks.

Challenge:

So, I challenge you today my young sister and my future leaders. Do not let what thorns (life happenings) that you may get stuck with cause you to "die empty". Do not let what thorns you have or may get stuck with deflate your dreams or the purpose that God has for your life. But, do remember this that some of these thorns will only just stick you and some will stay with you. Therefore, be it you just have a thorn in your side or you like me live in the "Briar Patch" don't let it stop you; don't let it get in your way. Because, just like the rabbit you were created to handle this.

Jane R. Coy

Arriving Virtuously

The wonder of it all is that as young ladies grow into womanhood they tend to suppose that their beauty is the key to a man's heart, a platform for getting an excellent job and reason of their happiness. However, I believe the greatest beauty secret that a woman can hold on too is - recognize who she is, loving herself and knowing that Jesus is her first love. The misconception of our beauty will cloud our thoughts and lead into our action. The Proverb 31 woman is a great example of a woman who understands who she is; a married woman, mother, hard worker, a helper, and a woman who loves the Lord.

I am that Proverb 31 woman. It took years for me to arrive at this place coming from Jamaica to a foreign land. Being kept back in school due to environmental change chock caused me to shut down. As I grew into womanhood, I got married at the age of 18 - the time when my peers and friends were enjoying their life; I had stepped into the world of responsibilities. In the mid-way, another hurdle came up I found out 5 years in the marriage I could not get pregnant. In spite of this, I kept on pushing until my perseverance finally paid off. Now I can truly say, I have been through the process and came out as a Proverbs 31' woman. I overcame the challenges of peers and bullying, graduated top of my class with my Bachelor of Art in Psychology and Counseling and got a Certification in Health and Weight Management as a Coach. My belief in God gave me a magnificent gift in 2012 in the form of a gorgeous baby girl name Chelsea. What the doctors' say was impossible; God said, "Mellisa, you are the Proverbs 31 woman and I will make your name great!"

Just like the Proverbs 31 woman's hard work for her family, I assuredly will say, this year, 2014, I will be able to retire my parents, give Chelsea the 'best' in her life and serve others in my community. In life you must have the perspective almost like the Proverbs 31 woman who says, "she is energetic and strong, a hard worker. She makes sure her dealings are profitable; her lamp burns late into the night" (Proverbs 31: 17-18). In life you must work hard for what you want! As you continue to work hard, do not forget to complete your schooling and build a business that will make your dealings profitable. Lastly, it may take time to create your dreams, however sooner or later it will be attainable. Just be willing to put some extra time in, even if you are working late all through the night. So, I challenge you; keep working hard while sharpening your talent. It is also known widely as you sow, so shall you reap. Just don't give up, because Greatness is in you!

Mellisa Lambert

A Daddy's Love

My story is far from roses and butterflies. I wasn't raised in a Christian home nor did our family attend church. My parents taught me right from wrong but there was no mention of Jesus or the Bible

Outside of that, I did have an awesome childhood full of love, laughter and memories. It wasn't until my teenage years that things got hard. Really HARD. My parents divorced when I was 12 and it turned my life upside down. Nothing made sense anymore. Life was out of control.

And I began to see my parents in a whole new way. Once two people who could rope the moon. Now they were flawed, imperfect and capable of hurt. I had spent so much of my life up to this point trying to please them and maintain this "good girl" image. But now as I sat all alone in my closet trying to make sense of the words I had just heard…"Me and your mom are getting a DIVORCE"

I just wanted to be someone else. I wanted to wake up from this nightmare and go back to my normal life. But it wasn't a dream. It was my life now and it was up to me to continue on this journey.

Much of which I would journey alone or so I thought...

I was 13 when the word "You are getting a little chubby" entered my world. Looking back I was nowhere near the description but coming from the lips of someone who promised to love me unconditionally. I knew it must be true. And so the vicious cycle of eating disorders began and its powerful grip would control my life for the next 15 years and at one point almost took my life altogether. I spent hours flipping through magazines and twisting and turning inspecting every inch and crevice of my body trying desperately to obtain that "perfect" image.

I was desperate to gain back some of the control I had seemed to have lost. My world was spinning and I just needed something to control. Something that was mine. Someone I could trust. Before my parent's divorce I had promised myself that I would wait until I was married to have sex. No one expected that of me, it was a promise I had secretly made to myself and one I held dearly. But after the divorce, it was almost as if there was no point in keeping this promise anymore.

And so I began the search of this unconditional love I had once known. I soon realized this "love" came at a price - A HUGE price. But I was desperate to be noticed. To be loved. That I paid that price and gave this sacred gift away so many times in hopes of receiving "love" in return. It never happened...

And I sunk deeper into depression and further into the darkness...

The darker my journey the more depressed I became. I was so intertwined in a web of drug abuse, partying and promiscuity that I had contracted two STDs and attempted suicide numerous times by the time I was 15 years old. My life was spiraling out of control and there was nothing I could do to stop it. And the darkness got darker...

One night I was invited to a party or what I thought was a party. It turned out to be a "private party" that consisted of me and two other guys. I was forced to do things that night that no one should ever be forced to do and it is only by the grace of God that I am alive to tell my story. I was ashamed, alone and afraid to share what really happened and so I hid my pain and tried to commit suicide numerous times following the attack. I was then admitted to a mental hospital and spent a week there. I wish I could say that it helped. It didn't.

It was a few months after I returned home that I began wanting more out of my life. I wanted out of the darkness. I wanted more. I wanted to believe I was MORE. And so I started praying (I still did not know the Lord at this point) for God to send someone into my life to help me, to guide me, and to teach me how to be a woman.

It wasn't long after that a lady showed up at my school appointed to be this deeply troubled girl's mentor. Every day she would come and listen to all my problems. She would encourage me and tell me that I was worthy, that I was loved, and that my life had value. It had been so long since I had heard those words spoken over me. Could it be true? I desperately wanted it to be...

She would also take me to these Christian women events; these women were so nice and loving towards me. And they talked passionately about their Jesus. That HE loved us UNCONDITIONALLY with a love that passionately peruses us no matter what darkness lingers in our midst. My heart leaped. THIS is what I had spent my whole teenage life searching for. Who was this Jesus they talked about? I was desperate to know.

My birthday was a few days later and my mentor sent me a balloon basket and inside was a gospel tract. And there all alone in my mom's apartment I laid all my sins, my darkest secrets, my hopes and dreams out on the floor and I cried out to this Jesus that I so desperately wanted to notice me and begged Him to save me and to help me see how this mess of my life could ever be fixed.

And notice me He did…He began to show me that He had always been perusing me in the darkest places with a love that I had never experienced before. He never once gave up on me. Never once looked away in disgust. As I sat all alone in that closet bearing the weight of those words…He was there whispering that it was going to be ok, that He was ever present in the midst of pain.

As I flipped through the magazines at the perfect images starting back at me… He was there whispering "My daughter, you are beautiful and you bear MY image." As I became intertwined in the darkness of drug abuse, promiscuity, rape, suicide attempts and depression. He was there whispering my child what Satan meant for evil, I intend for good. I WILL use this for my glory. As stared into the face of my newborn child while I too was still a child. He was there whispering I will never leave you nor forsake you. Do not fear or be dismayed. As that sweet mentor showed up in my life…He was there whispering I am you're TRUE friend, cast all your burdens upon me for my yoke is light.

And as I sat there in that empty apartment, begging Him to notice me …He was there whispering My child, You are My DAUGHTER. My BELOVED. You have WORTH. Your life has PURPOSE. You are FORGIVEN and I SEE you.   He pulled me up out of my slimy pit that day and has spent the last 16 years cleaning me off, healing my wounds, restoring my life and putting a NEW song in my mouth to encourage others for His glory.

And no matter what you are going through right now, know there is someone who is perusing you, whose love far surpasses any love the world has to offer. He is faithful to reveal you're TRUE: Beauty, Worth, Identity, Purpose and Purity. Seek Him in your pain. Seek Him in your imperfections. Seek Him in your darkness. He is ALWAYS there.

For I know the plans I have for you declares the Lord, plans to prosper you and not to harm you, plans to give you hope and a future.

Jeremiah 29:11

I waited patiently for the LORD; He turned to me and heard my cry, He lifted me out of the mud and mire: he set my feet on a rock and gave me a firm place to stand. He put a new song in my mouth, a hymn of praise to our God. Many will see and fear and put their trust in the Lord.

Psalm 40:1-3

Amanda Smith

Virtuous Wisdom

I have some wisdom to share and I stretch out my hand to you, for I have something you need. It's the wisdom I've acquired over my life and I want to give unto you what I have. My bounty is beyond anything bought with silver or gold. What I possess is priceless. I have acquired treasures galore. For me, it came with a great price, but it is worth the cost. We are not in this world for ourselves, but for others, to show forth the Love of the Father. Like Father, like daughter. I am so much like my Father, that is, Father GOD. "For God so love the world……..that He GAVE. I so love, therefore, I will so give.

A woman who walks with GOD should not be able to keep her treasure secret. She must share her wealth, her life experiences. Those valuable experiences have taught me many things that I can share with others and help them understand that they are not alone in their struggle, in their weaknesses, and in their transitions. Whether you need a hand to hold, an ear to listen, a heart to understand…..I am willing to be that for you. We must continue the tradition of becoming and being the Good Samaritan. We must become the ones who stop on our own way to be of assistance to someone who is struggling on theirs. The Love of GOD compels us to bind up their wounds, take them to safety and to show compassion upon them.

Women are created to function at a capacity that requires great faith, great strength, great power, and great authority and we should not function independently from one another. The Bible reminds us that we are our brother's keeper, and that goes for us women too. As Women of Faith, we must join the likes of Peter who responded in love to the lame man found at the gate of the temple. Peter said, "Silver and gold have I none; but such as I have given I thee: In the name of Jesus Christ of Nazareth, rise up and walk." GOD has granted us the same ability, to speak to one another and cause them to arise in strength and to walk in power. The total deliverance of this man was not just in the words Peter spoke, but in the action he took. The scripture confirms that Peter took the man by the hand, and lifted him up: and immediately his feet and ankle bones received strength.

If we are in relationship with Christ how can we not be in relationship one with the other? How can we not stretch forth our hands? The very word stretch means to exert effort, it's not always an easy thing to do. Stretching causes us to become uncomfortable in our created spaces, in our personal sanctuaries where we feel safe. Stretching will expose what's underneath the fancy clothes we wear, the makeup we apply, inside the cars we drive and in the beautiful homes in which we live. That's our fear....EXPOSURE! But, in that EXPOSURE there is the power to help others, and there in turn we will help ourselves.

While navigating through my toughest challenges I was hard pressed to find someone that was willing to help. Some of my greatest personal challenges I have faced alone, thinking no one understood where I was, or how I'd gotten there. I so needed just one person, just one, to look my way and help me. At first, it seemed that everyone looked the other way as if they didn't see me, or see my need. I am not sure if it was because what they saw was too painful to watch, or they didn't want to offer the help I needed because it would expose a part of them they wished to keep hidden. Perhaps they felt that I was strong enough to go it alone, or that I appeared to have it all together, when in fact, I was totally falling apart. Our smiles sometimes hide our needs. It sends a false message that all is well. We've learned to mask our internal conflict, and at all costs, never reveal our anguish. I was under what seemed like unbearable pressure.

We all have lived through some unpleasant moments and that should not be such a secret. After all, admission of our own imperfection releases us from a lie that pride will attach itself to and grow. The difficult personal situations I have lived through are great testimonies of the power of dependence on GOD and also on others around me. People never know your private struggle, they just judge your public strength. The two can be miles apart. If only we would respond in true love, willing to help and listen without judgment, maybe, just maybe, we then would become true Proverbs 31 Women.

"She stretched out her hand to the poor; yea, she reacheth forth her hands to the needy. "

Proverbs 31:20

No bad experience should hold us hostage; it should be turned into a learning experience for us and for those who will choose to listen to our stories. Giving to the needy is never all about material things, or money, but the riches of our personal experiences that hold life-giving information that we must be willing to share and release. As mothers, wives, homemakers, business owners, caregivers, you name it, women have many, many roles in today's world that makes a demand on her daily. At times we are depleted and in need of personal healing. We all should accept the awesome call of GOD to be helpers one of another.

GOD has always used relationship to empower man. Just as He created Adam and yet saw an incomplete being and was so moved that He lifted His voice and decided that man was not designed to be alone. Eve enters the story and GOD defined her role in that creative moment. Adam needed Eve, he was never meant to live alone, to carry weights alone, and to make decisions alone. He needed a partner and GOD created one made from the very rib of Adam himself. What an awesome responsibility, but having been created by the Hand of GOD, Eve was well equipped, and so are we.

There is nothing I have lived through, or anything I have acquired that I am not willing to share to see others benefit from lessons I've learned in my life. I will not fail to stretch forth my hand and reach out to help when what I possess can help. A Proverbs 31 Woman does this without hesitation.

Monica Cooper

Virtuously Bold

Since I was young, I've always battled with self-esteem. Something about me was never enough- too short, too quiet, too smart (wasn't cool enough). As I became older, those insecurities appeared in other aspects of my life. As a church musician, I wasn't skilled enough. As a wife, I wasn't pretty enough. As a mom, I could never do enough for my children. As a divorced parent, I felt like no man would want to deal with me because I had two children with a difficult ex-husband. Because of my deficiencies, I was content with being average.

In this scripture, Jesse brought to Samuel the sons that had "king potential" – looks, stature, experience in battle, etc. However, God was not satisfied with those sons. I'm pretty sure that Samuel was frustrated, too, since God didn't approve any of the sons that were present at the gathering. He was out of options, or so Samuel thought. Samuel asked Jesse if there were any more sons available. Jesse mentioned his youngest son, David, the "runt", was working in the fields. Samuel not only asked for David, but insisted on not doing anything else until David was in his presence.

God revealed to me that He will use the experience that you'd least expect to bring glory to His name. It's one thing to use the victories in your life to inspire others. I'm an accomplished teacher, musician, entrepreneur, and I've remarried. If anyone were to ask me to speak on these things, it would be easy because these experiences have brought great joy to my life. But what about those painful experiences or those experiences that didn't result in success? For me, I thought that God bringing me out of my divorce was enough; it was a painful experience and I had no desire to discuss it with anyone.

However, He's now using my divorce to bless others. I've remarried to a wonderful man who loves God unconditionally, which has made me comfortable to share the story of my first marriage. I've contributed one story to a book that will support abused women and I'm grateful for the opportunity to share my story with you in this book. In 2009, God gave me several songs that I simply jotted in my notepad or recorder on my phone's voice recorder. In January 2014, Apostle Candace Ford spoke over me that God desired me to be a David in the marketplace, to write and produce worship songs and financially support other artists in their calling to worship Christ in song. All of the phases of my life have prepared me to seek God, trust Him, and allow Him to elevate me.

Then Samuel asked, "Are these all the sons you have?"

"There is still the youngest," Jesse replied. "But he's out in the fields watching the sheep and goats."

"Send for him at once," Samuel said. "We will not sit down to eat until he arrives."
-1 Samuel 16:11

Don't be surprised when those experiences that you rarely think about suddenly come to the surface. God is seeking to transform lives with your testimony. Your life is not for you; you are a vessel! God will fill you and pour you into others throughout your life. People's lives are on hold and they're waiting on you to empower and ignite change so they can reach their God-ordained destination. I challenge you to be bold, step out on faith, and don't be afraid to meet a need with your story. God has graced you with a gift; trust

God to develop the gift in you and be ready for the call.

Sonja Jones

What seeds are you planting?

In 2009, a protective, sweet young girl was excited about celebrating her sister's birthday with extended family; when that excitement turned suddenly into fear because of an attack that could have cost her the preciousness of her life. Gratefully, the scares as permanent as they may be didn't break her of her love for others. The pit bull went after her as she distracted him from getting her little sister; tearing her leg to shreds but not her dreams.

Although the compensation her mother went after was for her injuries; it was also a down payment to her attaining her lifetime goals of ownership. Land, vehicles, and homes are at her disposal just for her picking. A young Proverbs 31 woman in her own rite; understanding the ability of prosperity verses poverty in her young age; I'm grateful to call this young woman my daughter.

> *"She picks out a field and buys it. She plants a vineyard from the profits she has earned. (Proverbs 31:16 GW)*

Lesson:

No matter the situation; find the positive in all things. We know that all things work together for the good of those who love God—those whom he has called according to his plan. (Romans 8:28 GW)

Challenge:

Look around and find at least three things positive about your day. Trust me it could be worst.

LaTracey Copeland Hughes

Strength and Honor

She shines bright like a diamond! My middle daughter, Razaria walks heavy in her anointing at such a young age. Strong and genuine in her gifts as she displays the love of God to all those in the land. She is talented beyond her years, but yet every good thing must come to an end. It's quotable," I'm going to be a singer and actress!" Believable yes, but I as her mother made her sit down for a season. Not because she wasn't talented but in every testimony comes a test.

> She dresses with strength and nobility, and she smiles at the future.
>
> Proverbs 31:25

A young Proverbs 31 woman with the smile to brighten any room; the light that draws you in was dim because of bullying and low self-esteem. Someone told her she wasn't the perfect size. Although she sang His praises daily she forgot one important thing.

I will give thanks to you because I have been so amazingly and miraculously made. Your works are miraculous, and my soul is fully aware of this. (Psalms 139:14 GW) She knew it, but didn't walk in that strength until today!

Lesson:

Sometimes we must be sat down in order to be brought up to our fullest potential.

Challenge:

Analyze talents in your life. Is there an area you could improve in because God said you could do just that? Write that promise down and never forget it!

LaTracey Copeland Hughes

Who is a Proverbs 31 Woman?

Hello, my name is LaTracey. That isn't who I am, but that is what they call me. It is not who "they" call you but what you've answered to, I was told. So, brace yourself for being naked is the only way you can fully understand who the Proverbs 31 Woman is. Evolution has begun from innocently being Ms. McDonald, beaten as Mrs. Olasande, neglected when Mrs. Copeland, falsely together yet abused Mrs. Bell, confused Mrs. Jacobs and currently the happy Mrs. Hughes.

If you've been single…I got you, married…I got you, divorced (even multiple times), abused, abundant and happily married, oh yes sister…I got you too! No honey, not arrogantly speaking; yet transparent because as the Proverb 31 Woman it takes a lifetime to achieve the commands of the woman of God.

I've been looking for love, attention, and affection from men whom I thought loved me. Multiple times, I was raped of my innocence very young but it never stopped my quest for success through my eyes. Only to realize that God could give me what I was searching for. Gracefully, I would walk through the doors of the church and smile publically as others thought this intelligent, youthful, risk taker was completely conquering the world, but it was all a joke.

When God called me and I answered; it wasn't always easy but doable. Only at that time, in summer of 2010 to be exact, did I decide to love myself more than I loved those men of my past. I was sent by God from Minnesota (the top) to Mississippi (the bottom) only to see that I could receive all that God had in store for me.

I still wasn't paying any attention to the promises of God until my daughters, who I was raising alone at the time, reminded me that the distractions kept me from all that God has for me. At that time, my oldest daughter brought my name, picture, and business card up to a saved, single hardworking man that wasn't my "idea" man. Only to my surprise, he was exactly the vessel that God used to show me His love.

Now sisters, you know when we are blessed with something good but not "packaged" the way we desire it, we disregard it? That is exactly what I did! Only to learn later about love, grace and mercy from God through him and that man is my husband today.

Preston loved me past my pain and never brought up one sin, or flaw of baggage that I carried into the marriage with me. Loving all of me and our children as his own; while supporting the woman of God that I have developed into.

Who is a Proverb 31 Woman, you ask?

It is I!

LaTracey Copeland Hughes the virtuous, noble, humble, wise, giving, faithful woman before you on today. I graciously hold my head up as I walk across stages, speaking on platforms that only God has prepared for me, encouraging other women like myself in which I have worn the shoes they are in. I am no longer ashamed of the rocks that you may decide to throw at me, for I have been under a huge bolder for years now.

I AM FREE!!! You may ask why I would keep a last name from my past to carry with me into my future. As I mentioned before, being transparent is the only way one can get healed. I held on to the name only because I began my professional career with that name. My past is just that "my past" and because of it I am standing before you Raising the Proverb 31 Woman.

~book excerpt from the upcoming book *Birthing Purpose by LaTracey Copeland Hughes*

Lesson:

No matter what I have been faced with I know that my redeemer lives within me. Continuing to hold my head up as I a woman of God no matter how bad things may be.

Challenge:

Sisters, I challenge you to look at your God given purpose in all situations and always remain a lady!

LaTracey Copeland Hughes

All About The Contributors
(more details on website)

www.RaisingAProverb31Woman.com

Aisha Z. Adams

Aisha Z. Adams is a wife and woman of faith. She is an author, inspirational writer, blogger and encourager. She wrote her first book "The Walk of Faith" in 2011 at a time in her life when her faith was being challenged. Website www.authoraishaadams.com

Facebook –Author Aisha Words of Encouragement and Inspiration

Twitter-@AuthorAisha   Blog – azainspirationalcorner.org

Deliela Watkins

Deliela Watkins is a Christian mother of three daughters. She strives to encourage young and mature women to be the best woman they can be and to trust God in every area of their lives. She is working on her first book that will be published this year and she currently resides in Cincinnati, Ohio.

Donna Rich

Donna Rich is a freelance writer, writing for Patch.org, online marketing reviews and blog. She recently coauthored a book, "Opening up to Life." She also works as a grant writer, helping non-profits in fund-raising, serves on a board of two nonprofits in process. She is in the process of opening up her parent coaching business and senior citizen concierge business.

Jacqueline Barnes

Jacqueline Barnes is the Founder of Seed of Hope Foundation a non-profit organization mentoring youth and young adults in Leadership Development and Life Skills. Her mantra to herself is, "The proof of desire is pursuit." Jacqueline serves as facilitator for Hope Center Workshops, and conducts professional life coaching sessions. Jacqueline currently resides in Illinois with her husband of 21 years Herman W. Barnes Jr., she has one daughter, Gwendolyn and three grandchildren; Jacquelynne, Jaymes and Justin.

www.mysoh.org

www.jacquelinebarnesministries.com

http://www.johncmaxwellgroup.com/jacquelinebarnes

Krissti Bryant

Krissti Bryant is honored to be Pastor, at Wall Less Ministries bringing a Ray of Hope™ to those in needs. Pastor Bryant teaches and preaches the infallible word of God. She is also a business owner and is currently authoring a book "Purpose by Design" that will be completed in 2014. Pastor Bryant is an encourager of women and is the Founder of Wall Less Women's Ministry.

www.walllessministries.com and www.purposebydesigllc.com.

LaShanna Watkins

LaShanna Watkins is a devoted and caring Woman of God. She teaches New Member's class alongside her Pastor. Her passion is teaching. She loves connecting with new members in the body of believers to help them feel welcome and to develop their purpose in the ministry. She is also married to a Man of God, Eugene Watkins and they live in Gulfport, MS.

Jane R. Coy

Jane Coy is a single mother of two boys (TySante age 17) and (Micah age 12). Jane is also taking part in a Midnight Inspiration call that happens on every Wednesday at 12 am and in the process of becoming a Co-author.

LaTrece Davis

Minister LaTrece Davis was born and raised in New Jersey but now resides in the state of Georgia. She was ordained a minister of the Gospel March 2012. She is founder of SALT Ministries which caters to young adults and singles. Her heart is in seeing the lost saved, the hurt healed, and the body of Christ walking in its rightful position.

facebook.com/basicministry and latrecedanyelle.blogspot.com

Lisa Johnson

Lisa Johnson, a very gifted singer/songwriter & performer, discovered her talent for writing and singing at the age of 7. She is the president of her own magazine entitled From Lisa's Corner THE MAGAZINE that interviews local businesses in the community as well as spotlight great talents such as singers, dancers, authors, poets, etc. For more information or bookings you may contact Lisa Johnson at:

Website: www.reverbnation.com/lisajohnson

ToyaSherie Gathings

"I Can Do All Things Through Christ Who Strengthens Me"
Philippians 4:13

LaToya Sherie Gathings born and raised in Chicago ,Illinois by way of Kankakee Illinois. I currently reside in Georgia where I am a Medical Dispatcher for one of the Top Rated Cancer Radiation Treatment Companies Varian Medical Systems Inc. Recent College graduate with an Associated Degree in Criminal Justice. Founder of Reign Beauty which will soon launch its release. Also still pursuing Modeling and an actress also hosting events. My most proud job is a mother of 2 beautiful daughters Shaiera Alexia and Zaria Sanaa Contact info toyasherie11@gmail.com

Renee Sunday

Renee' Sunday, M.D. is the founder and CEO of Sunday Publishing Company, LLC., and RS Commerce, P.C. Renee' is a radio and television personality, Grief & Loss Specialist , Group Counselor, Motivational & Inspirational Coach, Passion & Purpose Guru, Author, Publisher, Healthy coffee distribution owner, and an Anesthesiologist.

Tykeysha Boone

Ty has earned a Bachelor's of Science degree in psychology with a minor concentration in Community Health Education, she has a Masters of Public Health and is pursuing her Doctorate in Business Administration. Ty is published in a number of peer reviewed journals and other print media, and has held various leadership positions in both for-profit and nonprofit business sectors. Ty is an Independent Higher Education Professional, a Certified Nonprofit Consultant and a Wellness Strategist.

Contact Tykeysha at tykeysha@tybooneenterprises.com

Yvette L. Pye, Ph.D.

She recently published her memoir *"Going from the Projects to Ph.D.: Transcending My Geography."* In it she shares the journey of earning the Ph.D. and being at Saint Mary's despite being born in the projects, abandoned by drug addicted parents and being under prepared to do so. It is now available for purchase. Dr. Pye is available for speaking and teaching engagements and can be reached at: pye.yvette@gmail.com.

Candace Marquez

Candace Marquez presently works in Multi-Family Property Management, continuing her education by working toward a Master of Arts in Public Relations Spring 2014. Her career ambitions are to own a salon, pursuing her dream of directing her own scholarship pageant while perfecting her writing talents and motivational speaking.

Mellisa Lambert

As an Author, Motivational Speaker, Life, Business and Health Coach she is ready to impact her community at large. She is a self-help author that is determined to help those who are open for a change in their life. Mellisa's passion to inspire, motivate and help people to understand the power of their words; was revealed in her second book "Open Your Mouth and Speak 365 Positive Affirmations and Powerful Quotes".

Paula Foster

Paula Foster is a native of Atlanta, GA! Just as rare as it is to find a Georgia Peach, she is also a rare jewel. Paula is a visionary, mother, daughter, sister, aunt, domestic violence advocate and so much more! She is the founder of not one, but two businesses. They are Literary Giftings and Fostering Hearts. Literary Giftings is a for profit company for authors and entrepreneurs.

www.literarygiftings.com

www.fostering-hearts.org

Latasha Matthews

Latasha Matthews, Owner/CEO of IllumiNation Counseling and Coaching, LLC has worked in higher education and corporate America. She has provided in-home community-based therapy, and worked in a variety of private practice settings. She is well-versed in providing individual, couples, family and play therapy techniques. With over six years of experience as a marriage and family therapist, Latasha uses a Family Systems approach which considers how a particular system impacts an individual person or situation.

Sherry Turner

Sherry Turner is an education advocate for youth of all ages, through her field of education and psychology she teaches, mentors, counsels, and offer career placement via Leadership Youth & Community Center. Contact Sherry at sherryturner73@yahoo.com.

Alicia Hommon

Alicia Hommon is a daughter and worshipper of King Jesus, wife to Tracy, mommy to Clara, Elsie, and Ezra, and owner of Cake Whimzy. She has a degree from Fort Hays State University in music, and spent years pursuing what made "sense" in her life before finally submitting to what God created her to do. Her passion in ministry is twofold: first, through her business, no child, not one, would feel less than the treasure God created in them, and second, the Lord would continue to use her both nationally and internationally to light fires of intense love and worship for Jesus Christ in the marketplace.

Amanda Smith

Amanda Smith is daughter of the King, wife to her best friend of 13 years and homeschool momma of four kiddos. Amanda's passion to see teen girls discover their TRUE: Beauty, Worth, Identity, Purpose and Purity in Christ came from her own broken teenage journey. Amanda is living proof of a life that has been Redeemed. Restored and Remade for the glory of Christ. She is the founder of Broken Within Ministries where she helps girls see themselves through God's eyes instead of the worlds and gives them a voice in a culture where they are so commonly unheard. She provides them with a private Facebook group, Mentorship Program and Life Hurts, God Heals Recovery Groups. You can learn more about Broken Within here: www.brokenwithinministries.blogspot.com

Tymithia Davis

Tymithia Davis was born on July 26th 1989 in New Jersey to Sheila Davis and her late father Timothy Davis. She only has one sister, Latrece Davis. She came to know the Lord at a young age and is still in love with Him. She loves to write poetry, plays, books and whatever else the Lord puts on her heart to write. The Lord led her Georgia, where she now resides.

Montrice J. B.Littleton

Montrice J. B.Littleton is originally from New Orleans, LA. She relocated in Atlanta after surviving one of the biggest challenges of her life. She passionately shares her personal experiences and testimony in hope that someone will receive strength, peace, encouragement or revelation from God that they are not alone, that His love never fails and that He makes all things beautiful in His own time.

Minister Leslie Epps Wallace

Minister Leslie Epps Wallace is a licensed minister and has been sharing the gospel of Christ for over 8years. She is a motivational speaker, aspiring best- selling author, leader, teacher, and prayer warrior; Mrs. Wallace also walks in the office of the prophetic. She is currently starting a non-profit for displaced women. His Plans Ministry will be up on operating by the end of 2014. Above all of the titles, "I am a woman that loves God" and "His people". She loves sharing His word and helping others to know who they are in Christ. This is her passion, this is her purpose.

Trevva L. Douglas

Trevva L. Douglas is a wife and mother of one who has a deep passion for helping others. New to the journey of her purpose she is in the process of learning how to start her own business and plans to open a housing development for those who are without a home. With a "thing" for numbers she also hopes to increase her knowledge of financial literacy to be used to combat the mentality of poverty.

Monica Cooper

Monica Cooper is a poet and inspirational writer. Using writing as an outlet, Monica has written many inspirational stories, penned pearls of wisdom and communicated thought provoking works for many years. Her clever writing style is both educational and entertaining. She uses the pen name: The KINGdomDiva.

Lakita Stewart-Thompson

Lakita Stewart-Thompson is a servant of the Lord, visionary, mother, daughter, sister, community advocate, teacher, and writer. Raised in Maryland, Lakita is the Founder/President of Mothers & Daughters United Worldwide, which fosters "Better Bonds Between Daughters and Moms through serving communities together". Her ultimate desire is to have an organization that creates better situations for women, children, and families in need around the globe. She has a purpose to serve others through love, a passion to inspire the lost, and the heart of a philanthropist to give hope and help to the less fortunate. Lakita combined her passion, education, and experiences to create a charity based organizations.

Namaduworldwide.wix.com/namaduw-1

Sonja Jones

Sonja Jones is a "builder of lives". Before her roles of wife, mother, educator, musician, entrepreneur, leader, she is lover of God first. Her mission is to ignite growth in others by being a living testimony of God's goodness. Sonja's love for music has touched hundreds of lives in Memphis, TN through her piano studio, Music Is Piano Academy. You can contact her at www.sbjeducation.com.

Minister Kelley Sawyer

Minister Kelley Sawyer is an Author, Empowerment Speaker, Life Coach, Singer, Publisher, Certified IRS Tax Preparer, Entrepreneur, Wife, and Homeschooling Mother from the Chicago area. Though she wears many hats, her mandate is clear: to be an effective transformational life change agent in the body of Christ. She is the owner of Butterfly Methodz Press, A Christian Publishing Company, and is available to minister at your church and ministry experiences. She can be reached at 800.518.9730, Kelley@KelleySawyerMinistries.org, or by visiting her web site www.KelleySawyerMinistries.org. Minister Kelley is joyously married to the love of her life, George, and they have three beautiful children, George, Jr., Declan, and Abby.

About the Author

LaTracey Copeland Hughes is the president of Purposeful D.I.V.A. Enterprises, LLC as well as the CEO and Founder of Capstone Experience, Inc., 501c3, nonprofit organization that works with families that have youth in grades 6th through 12th in the areas of personal and academic goal setting around family involvement. LaTracey is a wife, mother of four, Publisher, Author, Business Consultant, Motivational Speaker, Minister, Certified Grant Proposal Writer, and Certified Life Coach.

La Tracey Copeland Hughes, The Purposeful Diva is a *divinely, inspired, visionary achiever* that will guide you to a better understanding of God's intended purpose for yourself, for us as His people, and for you as His unique creation. As you grow toward genuine peace and fulfillment, you'll learn the joy of loving God and others, waiting on Him with Hope, trusting Him through suffering, surviving in Him with reverent fear, and fulfilling His purpose.

Through her tests and trials birthed a transparent testimony that only God could create. He used her testimony and her past challenges to help others overcome their current circumstances. She currently coaches in the area of personal, spiritual growth and development, relational, and business-entrepreneurial success.

She uses the opportunity to coach in non-traditional facets such as social media, but also conferences, seminars, and writing. Mrs. Copeland Hughes is an expert in working with individuals that need someone to be non-judgmental while motivating, inspiring, and delivering them into their God ordained purpose by supporting them in the journey of discovery.

She received two Mini-MBAs in Non-Profit Management and Executive Leadership from St. Thomas University in Minneapolis, MN. She is married to Preston Hughes and is blessed to be the mother of Azuria aka "ReRe", Isaiah, Razaria, and Purpose.

All proceeds from this book will go to fund Capstone Experience, Inc., 501c3 nonprofit organization. Please visit www.capstoneexperience.org for more information or to donate.

Don't forget to visit our website for more information about the contributors and author. We are available for speaking engagements both virtually and in-person. Contact Purposeful Publishing and Consulting for more details www.RaisingAProverb31Woman.com email at latracey@latraceycopeland.com or call 530.205.3482.

www.ingramcontent.com/pod-product-compliance
Lightning Source LLC
Chambersburg PA
CBHW060520030426
42337CB00015B/1950